D1566267

Crime Prevention and Security Management

Series Editor
Martin Gill
Perpetuity Research
Tunbridge Wells, Kent, UK

It is widely recognized that we live in an increasingly unsafe society, but the study of security and crime prevention has lagged behind in its importance on the political agenda and has not matched the level of public concern. This exciting new series aims to address these issues looking at topics such as crime control, policing, security, theft, workplace violence and crime, fear of crime, civil disorder, white collar crime and anti-social behaviour. International in perspective, providing critically and theoretically-informed work, and edited by a leading scholar in the field, this series will advance new understandings of crime prevention and security management.

More information about this series at
http://www.palgrave.com/gp/series/14928

Russell Brewer · Melissa de Vel-Palumbo ·
Alice Hutchings · Thomas Holt ·
Andrew Goldsmith · David Maimon

Cybercrime Prevention

Theory and Applications

Russell Brewer
School of Social Sciences
University of Adelaide
Adelaide, SA, Australia

Melissa de Vel-Palumbo
Centre for Crime Policy and Research
Flinders University
Adelaide, SA, Australia

Alice Hutchings
Department of Computer Science
and Technology
University of Cambridge
Cambridge, UK

Thomas Holt
School of Criminal Justice
Michigan State University
East Lansing, MI, USA

Andrew Goldsmith
Centre for Crime Policy and Research
Flinders University
Adelaide, SA, Australia

David Maimon
Department of Criminal Justice
and Criminology
Georgia State University
Atlanta, GA, USA

Crime Prevention and Security Management
ISBN 978-3-030-31068-4   ISBN 978-3-030-31069-1   (eBook)
https://doi.org/10.1007/978-3-030-31069-1

Cover illustration: Przemyslaw Klos/EyeEm

This Palgrave Pivot imprint is published by the registered company Springer Nature Switzerland AG
The registered company address is: Gewerbestrasse 11, 6330 Cham, Switzerland

Series Editor's Preface

Russell Brewer, Melissa de Vel-Palumbo, Alice Hutchings, Thomas Holt, Andrew Goldsmith, and David Maimon present a critique of seven different types of commonly deployed crime prevention interventions which they believe have the potential to be used in tackling cybercrimes (with a specific focus on cyber-dependent offences). Certainly, for this reader, these distinguished authors have fulfilled their aim 'to make a substantial original contribution' as to how their chosen crime prevention techniques can be used to tackle offending in the digital realm.

Running through their analysis are at least three issues. The first is that cyber-offending and cyber-offenders typically have different characteristics to traditional offline offenders/offences. This complicates the potential application of traditional crime prevention approaches when applied to the digital arena. Second, there is a paucity of research, and in particular evaluations of these prevention approaches in the online world. The third point is that where there is evidence, it often produces mixed results—sometimes interventions work as intended, sometimes not, sometimes their effect is neutral, and sometimes they can make things worse. This book charts a path through these issues by critiquing the available evidence in the offline world, identifying relevant overlaps with activities online, and then exploring the potential for them to be so applied—providing guidance at the same time as to how this might be undertaken most effectively.

Taking situational crime prevention as an example, and there is more research on this approach than any other they discuss, evaluations suggest antivirus products are able at detecting and preventing malware attacks but are less positive about the effectiveness of warning messages in mitigating malicious hacking. The available evidence bars for other techniques such as firewalls, passwords, and security awareness programmes are far less developed.

Mass media messages such as awareness-raising campaigns are found wanting offline and have a limited applicability to online offending. Educational workshops may have potential although they will need a different orientation when applied in the cyber-world. Even good mentoring programmes can be thwarted by the difficulty of identifying relevant populations of both offenders and volunteers to help them. Targeted warnings and cautions by the police to warn potential offenders are deemed to have some potential where, for example, they focus on the wrongfulness of the act rather than the offender. Positive diversions that redirect offenders away from crime have some potential, for example, by transitioning malicious hackers to legitimate cybersecurity jobs. Restorative justice also has some appeal to victims and may help some offenders.

You will read more. The potential varies with offences and offenders and the context in which measures are introduced, but what is clear is that there is a need for more research. Offending has proliferated online because offences can generally be committed with more anonymity, where they have less chance of being identified, arrested, and successfully prosecuted and where victims are in plentiful supply. We know that policing generally and the security world specifically have struggled to keep up with changes, and this book suggests criminologists have too. Helpfully they outline in their final chapter ways of filling the knowledge gaps, both in terms of key issues to focus on and the positives and limitations of different evaluation methodologies.

This book is more than about cybercrime. It provides a critique and a review of crime prevention approaches and charts a way of better identifying how a much-neglected area of enquiry can be better understood, and, as importantly, how we can best target future prevention efforts. These alone make it an enticing read.

July 2019   Martin Gill

ACKNOWLEDGEMENTS

This work has its origins in a programme of research funded through the Home Office, which studied cybercrime prevention, knowledge, and practice. The book itself is an outgrowth from a symposium hosted by the University of Cambridge in late 2017, where the findings from this programme were presented by the authorship team. In bringing this research together here in this volume, we hope to contribute to the extensive work already being done by those within the cybersecurity community, law enforcement, and the criminal justice system, who contend with cybercrime and its impact every day.

The authors would like to acknowledge the contributions of several individuals, without whom this book would not have been possible. First and foremost, we would like to thank Catherine Schubert for her editorial and research support over the life of this project. Her patience, diligence, and good humour were greatly appreciated by all. We are also grateful to Ross Anderson, Alistair Beresford, Robert Clarke, Samantha Dowling, Richard Clayton, Sergio Pastrana, Daniel Thomas, and Julie-Anne Toohey for their inputs on earlier drafts of this work. In addition, we would also like to acknowledge the numerous scholars cited throughout the book, whose high-quality scholarship formed the basis of our evaluations and discussion. Finally, we would like to express our gratitude to Liam Inscoe-Jones, Josie Taylor, and the production staff at Palgrave for their dedication to bringing this book together.

In closing, the authors would like to acknowledge and thank the Home Office for funding the original programme of research, as well as the Centre for Crime Policy and Research at Flinders University for subsequent financial support in the preparation of the manuscript for this book.

Contents

LIST OF TABLES

CHAPTER 1

Setting the Scene

Abstract The book begins with an introductory chapter that sets the scene: providing an overview of the core principles associated with crime prevention targeting that will be drawn upon throughout. It chronicles the unique aspects of offending within digital contexts, and in particular, explicates offending lifecycles, and flags significant points of divergence from what is broadly accepted for offline forms of offending. Next, it provides a methodological account of the approach taken in researching this book, before concluding with an overview of chapters to come.

Keywords Cybercrime · Cyber-dependent crime · Cyber-offender · Crime prevention · Cybercrime prevention · Intervention

INTRODUCTION

Criminological research has made significant advances in the development, deployment, and evaluation of the myriad crime prevention strategies designed to identify and target individuals at various stages of the offending life cycle. This work, however, is principally rooted in understandings of what may be loosely called 'traditional' crime settings (Newman and Clarke 2003). Cybercrime is a relatively new crime type, and there has been little systematic attention given to the specific digital settings and contexts in which it occurs. As a result, many cybercrime prevention

© The Author(s) 2019   1
R. Brewer et al., *Cybercrime Prevention*,
Crime Prevention and Security Management,
https://doi.org/10.1007/978-3-030-31069-1_1

recommendations are not necessarily evidence-based. Such initiatives also tend to ignore the role of the offender (who can often displace to new targets or methods) and place the onus on victims to protect themselves. Scholars, practitioners, and policymakers are now seeking more effective ways to prevent cyber-offenders from attacking certain targets and to practically facilitate desistance from serious forms of cybercrimes. At present, they face a largely undeveloped theoretical and empirical body of literature.

Identifying and articulating evidence-based approaches to cybercrime prevention is critical due to the increasingly serious economic, national security, and political harms associated with the now-routine reports of compromised computer systems that have been used to access, reveal, or resell sensitive data (Franklin et al. 2007; Holt et al. 2016; Hutchings and Holt 2016; Motoyama et al. 2011). This book addresses this knowledge gap by investigating the applicability of evidence-based interventions to prevent cyber-dependent crimes. That is, crimes that can *only* be committed using a computer or network and include such acts as spreading viruses, malware, spyware, malicious hacking, and distributed denial of service attacks (DDoS) (McGuire and Dowling 2013).[1] These attacks have become a common global problem: in 2015, more than 1600 data breaches targeting governmental and private organisations exposed over 707 million records around the world (Gemalto 2015). Moreover, users of private computers, smartphones, and even medical devices increasingly report infiltration of their devices by illegitimate users (Storm 2015). This book adopts a broad definition of cyber-dependent crime that includes both 'illicit intrusions into computer networks', as well as the 'disruption or downgrading of computer functionality and network space' (McGuire and Dowling 2013, p. 4). Accordingly, the term 'cyber-offender' used throughout this book is also to be construed broadly—denoting those who use their knowledge to cause harm to, or directly damage, computer software, hardware, and data. This may include the use of malware (whether created by the individual or purchased/acquired from others) or exploits, or the manipulation of human actors to achieve said goals. This breadth is merited due to the range of interests and attack techniques that can be, and have already been,

---

[1] Such activities can be distinguished from cyber-enabled crimes which are regarded as 'traditional' crimes that are augmented through the use of computers or networking technologies (e.g. fraud) (McGuire and Dowling 2013).

used by individuals to successfully complete a cyberattack. Additionally, researchers have noted the overlapping interests and skills needed in order to write malware, engage in DDoS attacks on a fee-for-service basis, or complete malicious hacks more generally (Décary-Hétu and Dupont 2012).

Overall, the book aims to make a substantial original contribution to how the discipline of criminology understands and can reasonably apply longstanding, tried and tested, traditional crime prevention techniques to the digital realm, particularly for cyber-dependent crimes. In doing so, it breaks new ground and articulates the ways that crime prevention research and practice needs to be reimagined for an increasingly digital world.

This introductory chapter sets the scene for the book, providing an overview of the core principles associated with crime prevention targeting that will be drawn upon throughout. It chronicles the unique aspects of offending within digital contexts, and in particular, explicates offending lifecycles, and flags significant points of divergence from what is broadly accepted for offline forms of offending. Next, it provides a methodological account of the approach taken in researching this book, before concluding with an overview of chapters to come.

Approaches to Crime Prevention

In crafting any sort of preventative measure, be it on- or offline, it is important to first consider the point at which (i.e. when) an intervention is most suitable. Taking cues from an established public health literature, crime prevention scholars acknowledge that interventions can be designed to target different points (in this case, of the offending life cycle). These can broadly occur at one of three stages (Brantingham and Faust 1976). First, interventions can be designed to target the *primary prevention* stage, whereby they are intended to target and prevent criminal behaviour before it occurs. Interventions appearing at this stage are considered to be the most universal, being largely undiscriminating and targeted at wide populations. Such interventions tend to focus upon the earliest stages of the offender life cycle, before potential offenders begin engaging in criminal behaviours. Typically, interventions occurring at this stage involve reducing opportunities for crime, or enhancing social factors that reduce an individual's likelihood of becoming involved in crime. The next stage, classed as *secondary prevention*, is targeted towards people *at risk* of embarking on a criminal career, such as children who show some signs of delinquent behaviour. Such interventions, therefore, devote effort and resources towards those who may have an increased proclivity for criminal conduct, but before they graduate into more serious offending. Finally, the *tertiary prevention* stage focuses on treating individuals after they have become involved in crime. The focus at this stage is to prevent individuals reoffending. This is the most targeted level of intervention, by which individuals are formally referred to programming by the criminal justice system following a criminal conviction.

Determining the appropriate stage at which an intervention is to be directed can be based on several factors, including characteristics of the crime and the offender group, as well as more practical considerations such as resources. In particular, much research suggests the development of effective interventions relies on the accurate identification of factors known to contribute to offending (e.g. Bonta and Andrews 2017; Andrews and Bonta 2010; Andrews et al. 1990; Dowden and Andrews 1999; Koehler et al. 2013). Considerable research has been done to explicate such factors—particularly in offline settings. While criminogenic factors vary somewhat across different criminal populations (e.g. sexual offenders versus others), there is substantial overlap between categories, and correlates for criminal behaviour show many similarities for specific forms of criminal deviance (Bonta and Andrews 2017). The best-validated risk factors for criminal behaviour include: *individual factors*, such as being male and young, substance abuse, low educational achievement/unemployment, lack of structured prosocial leisure activities, antisocial personality patterns (i.e. impulsivity, poor problem-solving), antisocial cognition (i.e. attitudes/values/beliefs that promote criminal behaviour such as lack of empathy, pro-crime justifications, and anti-law attitudes); *family factors*, including coming from a low socio-economic status home, abuse and neglect, poor parental mental health, parental criminal history, parenting style, and parent–child relationship (i.e. harsh, lack of affection and supervision); and *social* factors, including urban environments, unstable living arrangements, and exposure to delinquent peers (for reviews see Cottle et al. 2001; Gendreau et al. 1996; Lipsey and Derzon 1998; Murray and Farrington 2010).

Factors Associated with Cyber-Dependent Offending

While cybercrime prevention literature is scant to date (Holt and Bossler 2016), there is a growing body of work explicating the offender characteristics for cyber-dependent crimes. This body of work flags a considerable departure from the above-mentioned broader literature and suggests that they exhibit distinctive demographic characteristics for which needs to be accounted. Particular characteristics of cyber-offenders may mean that interventions designed for other populations have different outcomes. For example, enrolment in education and employment reduces the likelihood of traditional offending, whereas it is not statistically significant in relation to cyber-offending (Weulen Kranenbarg et al. 2018). In fact, the relationship between education/employment and crime may be the inverse when it comes to cybercrime. Studies suggest that older offenders appear to be gainfully employed, working primarily in the computer security industry (Bachmann 2010; Schell and Dodge 2002), and many have completed education beyond high school (Bachmann 2010; Holt et al. 2008, 2009; Schell and Dodge 2002). In fact, said offenders tend to have a mix of both formal education and knowledge acquired on their own through reading and experiential learning (Bachmann 2010; Holt 2007). Empirical studies conducted on online communities of cyber-offenders (e.g. malicious hackers), however, suggest that offenders are predominantly under the age of 30 although there are older offenders as well working in the security community (Bachmann 2010; Gilboa 1996; Jordan and Taylor 1998; Schell and Dodge 2002). These younger people may be attracted to cyber-offending because they have greater access and exposure to technology, as well as the time to explore technology at deep levels.

There is also substantive evidence that like their offline counterparts, cyber-offenders have a number of social relationships that influence their willingness to engage in different forms of behaviour over time (Bossler and Burruss 2011; Holt et al. 2012; Leukfeldt et al. 2017; Skinner and Fream 1997). For cyber-offenders, online (or virtual) ties are critical in the formation of social networks and have been shown to serve as an essential source for technical expertise, tutorials, and malicious software tools (Décary-Hétu and Dupont 2012; Dupont et al. 2016; Leukfeldt et al. 2017). Such ties are utilised by cyber-offenders across the globe at every skill level and commonly manifest through widespread active and passive participation in Web forums, Internet Relay Chat (IRC), ICQ, and other forms of computer-mediated communication (CMC) (Holt 2009; Jordan and Taylor 1998; Skinner and Fream 1997; Leukfeldt et al. 2017). Starting first with networked bulletin board systems, and then later via Web forums, asynchronous CMCs have in particular (since the late 1970s), served as a key resource for information on systems and exploits, techniques on malicious hacking, as well as a potential source of co-offenders. Here, both new and experienced cyber-offenders post messages and respond to others and are often members of (or simply browse) multiple forums to gain access to these resources and people (Landreth 1985; Meyer 1989). In some cases, these forums are used as a means of connecting to others for the purposes of establishing formal malicious hacking groups (Slatalla and Quittner 1995). In addition to these online relationships, cyber-offenders often report close peer associations with individuals in the real world who are interested in malicious hacking (Holt 2009; Meyer 1989; Schell and Dodge 2002; Steinmetz 2015). These networks may form in schools or through casual associations in local clubs and national conferences (Holt 2009).

This body of research has important implications for the design and deployment of interventions for cyber-dependent crimes. While there exists a considerable empirical evidence base for various interventions across a number of offline contexts, given the divergent and distinctive criminogenic factors, its usefulness in preventing cybercrime is by no means assured. The coming chapters will shed light on this uncertainty by scrutinising this evidence base, and in so doing elucidate the applicability of such pre-existing intervention programs designed to deter offenders from engaging in cyber-dependent crimes.

Parameters of the Review

In order to address the aims and objectives outlined above in a systematic fashion, the review of evidence undertaken in this book adheres to strict criteria. First, for the purposes of this book, cybercrimes are strictly defined as cyber-dependent crimes (e.g. writing/distributing viruses and other malware, malicious hacking, DDoS). This book reviews available evidence for seven types of commonly deployed interventions for use in cybercrimes, selected for their potential applicability to cyber-offending. These include forms of Situational Crime Prevention (SCP) (Chapter 2), Universal Communication Strategies (Chapter 3), Educational Workshops (Chapter 4), Mentoring Programs (Chapter 5),

Targeted Warnings and Cautions (Chapter 6), Positive Diversions (Chapter 7), and Restorative Justice Practices (Chapter 8). Further discussion on each of these interventions and their applicability to digital contexts is provided at the end of this chapter.

This book considers evidence for the intervention as applied to cyber-offenders, and also by considering the evidence for the intervention as applied to individuals engaging in traditional crimes or delinquent activities. However, in assessing the relevance of the traditional crime research, populations that share characteristics with the proposed profile of cyber-offenders are given priority. Notably, and unless otherwise specified, the focus is on studies involving young people up to, and including, the age of 18 years. Extension beyond this age range is, however, justified where a paucity of studies directly arising from young people is encountered.

The evidence base examined in this book is inclusive of the international literature and works published after 1970. It considers only published empirical evaluation studies and systematic reviews found in articles, books, reports, and conference papers examining programs and initiatives undertaken in the context of the above seven named areas. This review is restricted to empirical studies written in English only. Given this limitation, it is likely that this review favours interventions designed, developed, and delivered in North America, Europe, and Australia/New Zealand. However, other regions are incorporated wherever data are available. It is worth noting that the majority of the evidence emanates from the USA, where evaluations of juvenile justice interventions are abundant. Given the scope of the aims and objectives proposed in this book, a wide range of empirical research (including studies using either quantitative or qualitative methods), encompassing a variety of study designs, are considered.

OVERVIEW OF THE BOOK

The chapters ahead explore the crime prevention interventions most commonly applied to crime problems. These include interventions specific to juvenile and young adult offenders, as well as changes to the environment in which crime may occur. We review their theoretical underpinnings and evidence for their efficacy. Most importantly, we consider their potential utility in the digital realm, given the unique features of the online environment. These main chapters are grouped together across four distinct parts.

Part I examines types of interventions that are directed at preventing criminal behaviour before it occurs—that is, at the *primary prevention stage*. To this end, SCP and universal communication strategies are explored.

Chapter 2 examines a broad range of techniques known as SCP. This form of intervention takes cues from a host of theoretical perspectives and involves the design and manipulation of the environment to make offenders' decisions to become involved in crime less attractive (Clarke 1995). The use of SCP is widespread in traditional contexts and is by far the most commonly deployed form of intervention in the prevention of cybercrime. Though extensive criminological research has found that SCP techniques can be successfully applied in traditional settings, it is still unclear whether SCP interventions can effectively prevent cybercrime. This chapter scrutinises available empirical evidence regarding the potential effect of SCP approaches (e.g. target hardening, surveillance, posting instructions) in deterring offenders from engaging in and escalating cybercrimes. It concludes by revealing the limitations of SCP in preventing cybercrime, as well as by elucidating the most promising configurations of SCP interventions in digital contexts moving forward.

Chapter 3 rounds out the first part of this book by exploring universal communication strategies: mass media messages that aim to deter people from considering or committing crimes. These interventions are underpinned by rational choice theories of crime (Cornish and Clarke 1986) and typically attempt to alter individuals' perceptions of the risks and rewards of offending. Mass media communications target a wide audience and have been traditionally applied to common crimes such as drink-driving. We consider the evidence, finding that overall there is very limited support for the effectiveness of communications at reducing offline forms of crime. Though universal communications have been applied to some extent in the digital realm, no evaluations have been conducted to assess their effectiveness. We describe the limitations of such strategies in digital contexts and provide a set of guidelines for design of communication strategies in this realm.

Part II of this book examines interventions consistent with the *secondary prevention stage*. That is, interventions that are targeted at specific individuals who may be at risk of engaging in serious forms of crime. To this end, we explore several interventions associated with this stage, including the use of educational workshops, mentoring programs, and the use of targeted cease-and-desist messaging.

Chapter 4 investigates the use of educational workshops in preventing crime. This type of intervention brings together groups of individuals deemed at risk of offending to educate them about the consequences of crime, or to promote positive behaviours and skills that reduce the likelihood of committing crime. Though educational workshops vary widely in terms of theory and content, most commonly they rely on social-cognitive theories of learning. School-based workshops have been applied extensively to combat illicit drug use, gang involvement, and general delinquency with varying success—some with positive effects, and some with negative effects. We conclude that workshops can be an effective way to reduce crime, but this depends greatly on the content and style of workshop deployed. However, to date, this strategy has not been widely utilised to deal with cybercrime, and consequently there is virtually no research on the success (or otherwise) of this strategy. We discuss the applicability of workshops in this space, explicating the features that would likely increase the success of this intervention in reducing cybercrime.

Chapter 5 examines interventions that can be broadly categorised as mentoring. Mentoring is underpinned by a philosophy that promotes supportive interpersonal relationships that offer guidance to young people throughout their social-emotional, cognitive, and identity development (Rhodes 2002, 2005). This chapter chronicles the popularity of mentoring as being one of the most commonly deployed interventions to prevent youth delinquency across traditional contexts, while at the same time drawing together a robust evaluation research literature that reveals only a modest-moderate effect associated with the intervention for those at risk of, or already engaged in, delinquency. Although to date, no research has examined either the utility or efficacy of mentoring as an intervention to target young people involved in cybercrime, we nevertheless argue that key lessons can be drawn from the extant offline crime prevention literature about future prospects in digital contexts. In making these arguments, we tease out the various factors associated with successful mentoring interventions and create a blueprint for the future design and deployment of such interventions.

Chapter 6 explores more coercive tactics, that involve the use of targeted warnings and cautions (i.e. cease-and-desist messaging) by police to warn potential offenders and deter them from future offending. These interventions rely on rational choice and labelling theories of crime. This chapter examines the results of studies that have evaluated such interventions for offline crimes, given the dearth of online evaluations. Overall, we find that most of the evidence indicates qualified support for the intervention. Although cease-and-desist visits and targeted prevention messaging have been used in the context of cybercrime, there is little known about how effective they are. In exploring the applicability of these interventions to cybercrime, we highlight their limitations within digital contexts and provide recommendations for optimal design of this strategy for preventing cybercrime.

Part III of this book explores interventions aligning with the *tertiary prevention stage*. As described above, such interventions focus on treating individuals after they have become involved in crime, so as to prevent them from reoffending. Here we explore the use of several prominent forms of programming following a criminal conviction, including the use of various positive diversions, as well as restorative justice practices.

Chapter 7 examines the use of positive diversions in reducing crime. Positive diversions attempt to avoid the criminogenic effect of traditional criminal justice procedures (e.g. via labelling and/or peer contagion) by replacing these procedures with rehabilitative or prosocial activities (e.g. arts, education, sporting activities). This chapter reviews the evidence for such interventions, concluding that the findings are mixed, with some diversions showing positive effects and others showing negative effects. We then explore the applicability of positive diversions to cybercrime, finding that although there is no research evidence for their effectiveness, there is some anecdotal evidence that redirecting cyber-offenders into cybersecurity programs or training could be beneficial. We conclude by discussing what an ideal positive diversion program would look like for cyber-offenders, drawing out the factors that would likely lead to its success in the digital realm.

Chapter 8 investigates a series of interventions that fall under the banner of restorative justice procedures. These procedures offer an informal alternative to formal court processes and typically involve bringing the offender and the victim together to discuss the harm caused, as well as measures to remediate the harm and assist the offender to avoid future offending. Restorative justice is influenced by re-integrative shaming theory (Braithwaite 1989), which argues that holding offenders accountable for their crimes in a socially re-integrative way can facilitate reconciliation and healing. We review the research literature, finding that the evidence for restorative justice interventions in reducing recidivism for traditional crimes is mixed, and overall, weak. To date, there are no studies that have empirically assessed the use of restorative justice practices in relation to cybercrimes of any kind, though some scholars have speculated as to their potential applicability. We outline the difficulties of applying restorative justice interventions to the online context and formulate a proposal for best-practice restorative justice procedures for cybercrime.

Part IV of this book contains the final chapter (Chapter 9) which, draws together the key empirical strands that have emerged throughout and explicates the practical dimensions of this work. It acknowledges first, that there has been very little research evaluating the effects of crime prevention initiatives on cybercrime. It then outlines ways in which this gap can be addressed in the future, and some of the issues that both researchers and practitioners will need to be aware of when it comes to implementing and evaluating cybercrime interventions. This chapter concludes by offering a number of recommendations for practitioners and researchers seeking to evaluate cybercrime interventions in the future.

References

Andrews, D. A., & Bonta, J. (2010). Rehabilitating criminal justice policy. *Psychology, Public Policy, and Law, 16,* 39–55. https://doi.org/10.1037/a0018362.

Andrews, D. A., Zinger, I., Hoge, R. D., Bonta, J., Gendreau, P., & Cullen, F. T. (1990). Does correctional treatment work? A clinically relevant and psychologically informed meta-analysis. *Criminology, 28,* 369–404. https://doi.org/10.1111/j.1745-9125.1990.tb01330.x.

Bachmann, M. (2010). The risk propensity and rationality of computer hackers. *The International Journal of Cyber Criminology, 4,* 643–656.

Bonta, J., & Andrews, D. A. (2017). *The psychology of criminal conduct* (6th ed.). New York, NY: Routledge.

Bossler, A. M., & Burruss, G. W. (2011). The general theory of crime and computer hacking: Low self-control hackers? In T. J. Holt & B. H. Schell (Eds.), *Corporate hacking and technology-driven crime: Social dynamics and implications* (pp. 38–67). Hershey, PA: IGI Global. https://doi.org/10.4018/9781616928056.ch003.

Braithwaite, J. (1989). *Crime, shame and reintegration.* Cambridge, UK: Cambridge University Press. https://doi.org/10.1017/cbo9780511804618.

Brantingham, P. J., & Faust, F. L. (1976). A conceptual model of crime prevention. *Crime & Delinquency, 22*(3), 284–296. https://doi.org/10.1177/001112877602200302.

Clarke, R. V. (1995). Situational crime prevention. *Crime and Justice, 19,* 91–150. https://doi.org/10.1086/449230.

Cornish, D. B., & Clarke, R. V. (1986). Rational choice approaches to crime. In D. B. Cornish & R. V. G. Clarke (Eds.), *The reasoning criminal: Rational choice perspectives on offending* (pp. 1–16). New York, NY: Springer-Verlag.

Cottle, C. C., Lee, R. J., & Heilbrun, K. (2001). The prediction of criminal recidivism in juveniles: A meta-analysis. *Criminal Justice and Behavior, 28,* 367–394. https://doi.org/10.1177/0093854801028003005.

Décary-Hétu, D., & Dupont, B. (2012). The social network of hackers. *Global Crime, 13*(3), 160–175. https://doi.org/10.1080/17440572.2012.702523.

Dowden, C., & Andrews, D. A. (1999). What works in young offender treatment: A meta-analysis. *Forum on Corrections Research, 11,* 21–24.

Dupont, B., Côté, A.-M., Savine, C., & Décary-Hétu, D. (2016). The ecology of trust among hackers. *Global Crime, 17*(2), 129–151. https://doi.org/10.1080/17440572.2016.1157480.

Franklin, J., Paxson, V., Perrig, A., & Savage, S. (2007, October). *An inquiry into the nature and cause of the wealth of Internet miscreants.* Paper presented at CCS '07, Alexandria, VA.

Gemalto. (2015). *First half review: Findings from the breach level index.* Retrieved from https://www.gemalto.com/brochures-site/downloadsite/Documents/Gemalto_H1_2015_BLI_Report.pdf. Accessed 26 June 2019.

Gendreau, P., Little, T., & Goggin, C. (1996). A meta-analysis of the predictors of adult offender recidivism: What works! *Criminology, 34*(4), 575–608. https://doi.org/10.1111/j.1745-9125.1996.tb01220.x.

Gilboa, N. (1996). Elites, lamers, narcs, and whores: Exploring the computer underground. In L. Cherny & E. R. Weise (Eds.), *Wired women* (pp. 98–113). Seattle, WA: Seal Press.

Holt, T. J. (2007). Subcultural evolution? Examining the influence of on- and off-line experiences on deviant subcultures. *Deviant Behavior, 28,* 171–198. https://doi.org/10.1080/01639620601131065.

Holt, T. J. (2009). Lone hacks or group cracks: Examining the social organization of computer hackers. In F. Schmalleger & M. Pittaro (Eds.), *Crimes of the Internet* (pp. 336–355). Upper Saddle River, NJ: Pearson Prentice Hall.

Holt, T. J., & Bossler, A. M. (2016). *Cybercrime in progress: Theory and prevention of technology-enabled offenses.* London, UK: Routledge.

Holt, T. J., Bossler, A. M., & May, D. C. (2012). Low self-control, deviant peer associations, and juvenile cyberdeviance. *American Journal of Criminal Justice, 37,* 378–395. https://doi.org/10.1007/s12103-011-9117-3.

Holt, T. J., Kilger, M., Strumsky, D., & Smirnova, O. (2009, July). *Identifying, exploring, and predicting threats in the Russian hacker community.* Paper presented at the DefCon 17 Convention. Las Vegas, NV.

Holt, T. J., Smirnova, O., & Chua, Y. T. (2016). Exploring and estimating the revenues and profits of participants in stolen data markets. *Deviant Behavior, 37*, 353–367. https://doi.org/10.1080/01639625.2015.1026766.

Holt, T. J., Soles, J., & Leslie, L. (2008, April). *Characterizing malware writers and computer attackers in their own words.* Paper presented at the 3rd International Conference on Information Warfare and Security, Omaha, NE.

Hutchings, A., & Holt, T. J. (2016). A crime script analysis of the online stolen data market. *British Journal of Criminology, 55*, 596–614. https://doi.org/10.1093/bjc/azu106.

Jordan, T., & Taylor, P. (1998). A sociology of hackers. *The Sociological Review, 46*, 757–780. https://doi.org/10.1111/1467-954X.00139.

Koehler, J. A., Lösel, F., Akoensi, T. D., & Humphreys, D. K. (2013). A systematic review and meta-analysis on the effects of young offender treatment programs in Europe. *Journal of Experimental Criminology, 9*, 19–43. https://doi.org/10.1007/s11292-012-9159-7.

Landreth, B. (1985). *Out of the inner circle.* Seattle, WA: Microsoft Press.

Leukfeldt, R., Kleemans, E. R., & Stol, W. (2017). Origin, growth, and criminal capabilities of cybercriminal networks: An international empirical analysis. *Crime, Law and Social Change, 67*, 39–53. https://doi.org/10.1007/s10611-016-9663-1.

Lipsey, M. W., & Derzon, J. H. (1998). Predictors of serious delinquency in adolescence and early adulthood: A synthesis of longitudinal research. In R. Loeber & D. P. Farrington (Eds.), *Serious and violent offenders: Risk factors and successful interventions* (pp. 86–105). Thousand Oaks, CA: Sage. https://doi.org/10.4135/9781452243740.n6.

McGuire, M. & Dowling S. (2013). *Cyber crime: A review of the evidence* (Home Office Research Report No. 75).

Meyer, G. R. (1989). *The social organization of the computer underground.* Master's thesis. Retrieved from the National Institute of Standards and Technology Computer Security Resource Center (ADA390834).

Motoyama, M., McCoy, D., Levchenko, K., Savage, S., & Voelker, G. M. (2011, November). An analysis of underground forums. In *Proceedings of the 2011 ACM SIGCOMM Internet Measurement Conference* (pp. 71–80). New York, NY: ACM.

Murray, J., & Farrington, D. P. (2010). Risk factors for conduct disorder and delinquency: Key findings from longitudinal studies. *The Canadian Journal of Psychiatry, 55*, 633–642. https://doi.org/10.1177/070674371005501003.

Newman, G., & Clarke, R. (2003). *Superhighway robbery: Preventing e-commerce crime.* Cullompton, NJ: Willan Press. https://doi.org/10.4324/9781843924876.

Rhodes, J. E. (2002). *Stand by me: The risks and rewards of mentoring today's youth.* Cambridge, MA: Harvard University Press.

Rhodes, J. E. (2005). A model of youth mentoring. In D. L. DuBois & M. J. Karcher (Eds.), *Handbook of youth mentoring* (pp. 30–43). Thousand Oaks, CA: Sage. https://doi.org/10.4135/9781412976664.n3.

Schell, B. H., & Dodge, J. L. (2002). *The hacking of America: Who's doing it, why, and how.* Westport, CT: Quorum.

Skinner, W. F., & Fream, A. M. (1997). A social learning theory analysis of computer crime among college students. *Journal of Research in Crime and Delinquency, 34,* 495–518. https://doi.org/10.1177/0022427897034004005.

Slatalla, M., & Quittner, J. (1995). *Masters of deception: The gang that ruled cyberspace.* New York, NY: HarperCollins.

Steinmetz, K. F. (2015). Craft(y)ness: An ethnographic study of hacking. *British Journal of Criminology, 55,* 125–145. https://doi.org/10.1093/bjc/azu061.

Storm, D. (2015, June 8). *MEDJACK: Hackers hijacking medical devices to create backdoors in hospital networks.* Computerworld. Retrieved from https://www.computerworld.com/article/2932371/medjack-hackers-hijacking-medical-devices-to-create-backdoors-in-hospital-networks.html. Accessed 26 June 2019.

Weulen Kranenbarg, M., Ruiter, S., van Gelder, J.-L., & Bernasco, W. (2018). Cyber-offending and traditional offending over the life-course: An empirical comparison. *Journal of Developmental and Life-Course Criminology, 4*(3), 343–364. https://doi.org/10.1007/s40865-018-0087-8.

Primary Forms of Prevention

CHAPTER 2

Situational Crime Prevention

Abstract This chapter examines a broad range of techniques known as situational crime prevention (SCP). This form of intervention takes cues from a host of theoretical perspectives and involves the design and manipulation of the environment to make offenders' decisions to become involved in crime less attractive. The use of SCP is widespread in traditional contexts and is by far the most commonly deployed form of intervention in the prevention of cybercrime. Though extensive criminological research has found that SCP techniques can be successfully applied in traditional settings, it is still unclear whether SCP interventions can effectively prevent cybercrime. This chapter scrutinises available empirical evidence regarding the potential effect of SCP approaches (e.g. target hardening, surveillance, posting instructions) in deterring offenders from engaging in and escalating cybercrimes. It concludes by revealing the limitations of SCP in preventing cybercrime, as well as by elucidating the most promising configurations of SCP interventions in digital contexts moving forward.

Keywords Antivirus software · Computer monitoring ·
Computer surveillance · Malicious software ·
Situational crime prevention · Warning messages

R. Brewer et al., *Cybercrime Prevention*,
Crime Prevention and Security Management,
https://doi.org/10.1007/978-3-030-31069-1_2

INTRODUCTION

In order to facilitate safe and secure Internet infrastructures, many corporations and individuals use technical tools and security policies that aim to configure the online environment in such a way that reduces the probability of cybercrime from occurring or progressing. For instance, firewalls and intrusion detection/prevention systems are commonly used by large organisations to prevent the progression of cybercrime (Bace and Mell 2001). Similarly, one important policy often incorporated into contemporary computing environments is the implementation of surveillance means in users' computer systems (Eivazi 2011). These and other approaches to prevent the development of cybercrime coincide with the list of crime prevention strategies that are recommended by the situational crime prevention (SCP) perspective (Homel and Clarke 1997; Cornish and Clarke 2003), originally designed to prevent the occurrence of offline crimes.

In this chapter, we explore the theoretical underpinnings of the SCP approach to crime prevention and details how this suite of techniques has been applied in both offline and digital contexts. We then scrutinise the available empirical evidence regarding the potential effect of SCP approaches in deterring cyber-offenders from engaging in or escalating their criminal activities. Despite the growing number of individuals and organisations that implement these tools and policies on their computing environments, the effectiveness of these strategies in preventing and mitigating the occurrence of malicious cyber activities is limited. This chapter concludes by revealing the limitations of SCP in preventing cybercrime, as well as by elucidating the most promising configurations of SCP interventions in digital contexts moving forward.

THEORETICAL UNDERPINNINGS OF THE INTERVENTION

The SCP perspective (Clarke 1995) is focused on the occurrence and development of criminal events. The underlying premise of this perspective is that criminals are rational creatures who weigh the costs and benefits of their behaviours, so successful crime prevention efforts must involve the design and manipulation of human environments to make offenders' decisions to become involved in crime less attractive (Clarke 1995). Emphasising the centrality of offenders' decision-making processes in determining involvement in deviance and crime,

Clarke (1995) differentiated between individual decisions to become involved in crime (i.e. criminal involvement) and decisions to become involved in a particular criminal event. According to Clarke (1995), individuals first decide whether they are willing to become involved in crime in the first place. This decision is largely influenced by past learning and experiences (including one's moral code) and a range of background characteristics (demographic and social). Once the choice to get involved in crime is made, individuals need to decide whether to commit particular offences. This decision is largely determined by the immediate situations and criminogenic opportunities individuals encounter.

Importantly, Clarke (1995) acknowledged the prevalence of situations conducive to crime in the lives of most people, and the commission of risky behaviours and illegal acts by both 'ordinary citizens' and 'hardened offenders'. Incorporating this insight with the notion that the decision to initiate a risky behaviour is induced by the absence of moral opprobrium attached to criminal opportunities, Clarke (1995) contended that both property and violent offences may be effectively prevented by reducing the opportunity for criminal events and deterring offenders from violating the law. Therefore, Clarke (1995) recommended the adoption of crime-specific prevention strategies (e.g. strategies targeting theft, robbery, burglary, vandalism, etc.) that fall into five categories: (1) increase offenders' effort; (2) increase offenders' risks; (3) reduce offenders' rewards; (4) reduce provocations; and (5) remove excuses (Cornish and Clarke 2003).

Current Applications

SCP approaches have also been used extensively in the offline or 'traditional' contexts. In fact, many of the 25 techniques discussed in Cornish and Clarke's (2003) elaboration of the SCP perspective have proven useful in reducing different types of offline crime. For example, after reviewing a set of 41 studies, Welsh and Farrington (2008a) reported that CCTV cameras were effective in reducing vehicle crimes, consistent with the SCP strategy that calls for increasing formal surveillance. Welsh and Farrington (2008b) further reported that improved street lighting significantly reduces the probability of crime in public space, consistent with the SCP strategy that calls for assisting natural surveillance. Similarly, after reviewing evidence from 19 studies, Bennett et al. (2009) reported that neighbourhood watches are effective in reducing crimes in residential communities, consistent with the SCP strategy that calls for extending guardianship. Finally, several studies suggest that warning signs are effective in deterring claim padding of insured persons (Blais and Bacher 2007) and unsafe driving (Rama and Kulmala 2000).

While these studies and systematic reviews present evidence regarding the effectiveness of these specific SCP techniques in preventing crime, extensive criminological literature extends anecdotal evidence regarding the potential of these and other techniques in preventing a wide range of crimes, including aircraft hijackings, robbery (Crow and Bull 1975; Scott et al. 1985; Jeffrey et al. 1987), vandalism (Sloan-Howitt and Kelling 1990), adolescent joyriding (Bell and Burke 1992), and shoplifting (Farrington 1993). For a comprehensive review of the effectiveness of SCP techniques in preventing different types of crimes, see Crawford and Evans (2017), Guerette and Bowers (2009), and Cozens et al. (2005).

The growing volume of cybercrime incidents during the last fifteen years has led criminologists and information scientists around the world to explore effective ways of preventing cyber-offenders from victimising individuals and large organisations. Many scholars have examined the utility of the 25 SCP techniques in preventing different types of cybercrime. These interventions manifest as a number of distinct forms that include the use of firewalls (e.g. Lyu and Lau 2000; Surisetty and Kumar 2010), antivirus programs (e.g. Algaith et al. 2016; Lévesque et al. 2013, 2016), intrusion detection or prevention systems (e.g. Faysel and Haque 2010; Seeberg and Petrovic 2007; Garg et al. 2006; Lévesque and Fernandez 2014), vulnerability patching (e.g. Dacey 2003; Gerace and Cavusoglu 2009; Korman et al. 2017; Nayak et al. 2014), warning messages (e.g. Maimon et al. 2014; Testa et al. 2017), the use of passwords (e.g. Bonneau 2012; Cazier and Medlin 2006; Florêncio et al. 2016), police crackdowns (see Décary-Hétu and Giommoni 2017), honeypots (see Algaith et al. 2016; Kambow and Passi 2014; Ramsbrock et al. 2007), surveillance in computers (e.g. Eivazi 2011; Wilson et al. 2015), audit trails (e.g. Berlin et al. 2015; Guttman and Roback 1995), website takedowns (e.g. Hutchings et al. 2016), fraud detection systems, and spam filtering (e.g. Hutchings et al. 2019).

EVIDENCE BASE FOR THE INTERVENTION

Given the burgeoning interest in SCP and the extent to which such strategies have been deployed in preventing cybercrime, there is a small but growing experimental and quasi-experimental evidence base demonstrating its effectiveness as an intervention. These scientific evaluations use methodologically robust research designs (see further Chapter 9) to draw conclusions about the effectiveness of some of the above-mentioned interventions in preventing and mitigating cybercrime—particularly via the use of antivirus software, and the deployment of warning messages, as well as the use of monitoring and surveillance systems. This evidence base will now be canvassed.[1]

First, *Antivirus software* programs are designed to keep computer devices clean from malicious software (malware) such as viruses, worms, and trojans (Sukwong et al. 2011) and are commonly deployed on computer and smartphone users' devices as the last line of defence against cybercrime (Algaith et al. 2016). In general, several key approaches are employed by scholars when evaluating the performance of antivirus software. The typical evaluations conducted by commercial and scholarly labs are based on scans of collected or synthesised malware samples (PC Security Labs 2013; Algaith et al. 2016; Bishop et al. 2011). While this approach may test the program's accuracy, it fails to consider computer users' behaviours with their computers. An alternative approach for evaluating antivirus software performance is through the use of an on-demand detection tool that can detect both the presence of threats on the scanned computer and the availability of antivirus software (AV Comparatives 2011). Although informative, these studies are subject to sample selection bias because the samples they employ include computer users who bought the scanning service only. Another approach for assessing the effectiveness of antivirus software employs computer users' self-reports on security incidents they experience with their computers, as well as reports on the presence of antivirus software on their computers (Eurostat 2011). Unfortunately, these studies draw on survey

[1] It is important to note that evidence reviewed did not include findings which reported results of scans performed under lab conditions (of either collected or synthesised samples of attacks). Although valuable for providing insights regarding specific features of these tools and policies, these examinations are not representative of real-life situations since they do not account for human, organisational, environmental, and other external factors that may influence the performance and execution of these tools in the field.

methodology and may include multiple inaccuracies. Finally, two recent studies (Lévesque et al. 2013, 2016), described below, employed trials to assess the effectiveness of antivirus products in detecting and preventing malware infections among computer users.

In 2013, Lévesque et al. provided 50 participants with new laptops and monitored their real-world computer usage via various diagnostic tools over a period of four months. These scholars also conducted monthly interviews with the participants and administered questionnaires among them. The authors reported that during the four months of the experimental period, 38% of the study participants were exposed to malware. Accordingly, the authors suggest that almost 1 out of 2 newly installed laptops would have been infected with malware within 4 months if the computers had no antivirus software installed. In addition to determining the overall exposure to malware infection, the authors also explored the proportion of malware infections that went undetected by the antivirus software during the experimental period. They reported that 20% of the study computers were infected by some form of malicious software that was not detected by the antivirus software that was installed on the machine.

In their second and more extensive investigation, Lévesque et al. (2016) reported on a large-scale cohort study that was aimed to test the effectiveness of different antivirus products in detecting and preventing malware infections. Using data collected from millions of computers that had the *Microsoft Malicious Software Removal Tool* and *Microsoft Windows Defender* (Microsoft's default antivirus software) installed, these scholars reported results from a natural experiment: malware infection was the outcome and being protected by a third-party antivirus product was the exposure measure. Specifically, by monitoring close to 27 million *Windows 10* systems for a period of 4 months, the scholars were able to differentiate between systems that were protected by third-party antivirus products (the treatment group) and systems that were protected by *Microsoft Windows Defender*, the control group. Using this data, they tested the probability of these computers to become infected with malware. The authors found that 1.22% of the computer systems in the experimental group were infected by malware during the experimental period. In contrast, 14.95% of the computer systems in the control group could have been infected by malware if no antivirus products were protecting them. A comparison of the effectiveness of the 10 most prevalent antivirus products (more than 90% of the systems were protected by third-party software) revealed that the effectiveness of these products in detecting malicious software ranged from 90 to 98%. In summary, antivirus programs appear to be an effective strategy for discovering and preventing against malware infection, providing that the malicious software signature is already updated in the antivirus software's database of malicious signatures.

Warning messages are intended to modify people's behaviours and serve as reminders about the hazards involved in a particular action (Wogalter 2006). We review *targeted warnings and cautions* in Chapter 6—that is, warnings delivered by law enforcement personnel to identify individuals who have engaged in criminal activity or are likely to do so in future. In contrast, here we review generic warning messages that are more closely aligned with the SCP perspective. That is, messages displayed by automated software to offenders in situ (i.e. the online space as the potential crime is occurring) that are designed to prevent the commission of the crime or reduce its severity. Maimon et al. (2014) investigated the effect of a warning banner on the progression, frequency, and duration of system trespassing events. To test their research questions, the researchers deployed a large set of target computers built for the sole purpose of being attacked (i.e. honeypots), on the Internet infrastructure of a large American university. They then conducted two randomised experiments. In both experiments, the target computers (86 computers in the first experiment and 502 computers in the second) were set to either display or not display a warning banner once system trespassers had successfully infiltrated the systems. Findings from these two experiments reveal that a warning banner did not lead to the immediate termination or a reduction in the frequency of trespassing incidents. Nevertheless, the duration of system trespassing incidents recorded on target computers with a warning banner was significantly shorter than those recorded on target computers with no-warning banners. These differences were observed for both the first system trespassing incidents recorded on each of the target computers and for the overall set of incidents recorded during the experimental period. Moreover, these authors reported that the effect of a warning message on the duration of repeated trespassing incidents was attenuated in computers with a large bandwidth capacity. A later study replicated Maimon et al.'s (2014) finding that mean duration of a system trespassing event was significantly shorter with a warning, than under the no-warning condition (Stockman et al. 2015).

Using the data collected by Maimon et al. (2014), Testa et al. (2017) explored the effect of a warning on mitigating trespassers' levels of activity in an attacked computer system. These scholars reported three key findings. First, the presence of a warning banner on an attacked computer system had no statistically significant effect on the probability of either navigation or 'change file permission' commands being entered on the system. Second, the presence of a warning banner did not affect either the probability or the average rate of navigation commands being entered on computers infiltrated by system trespassers with administrative privileges. However, the presence of a warning banner significantly increased the proportion of target computers with 'change file permission' commands. Specifically, while 52% of the warning target computers attacked by an administrative system trespasser recorded the 'change file permission' command, only 39% of the no-warning target computers that were attacked by administrative system trespassers recorded a 'change file permission' command. Moreover, the average rate of 'change file permission' commands entered on the warning target computers was significantly higher than the average rate of 'change file permission' commands on no-warning computers. In contrast, these authors reported that a warning banner substantially reduced the use of both navigation and 'change file permission' commands on computers attacked by system trespassers with non-administrative privileges.

Jones et al. (2016) explored what type of warning message—sanction threats or moral persuasion—were more effective in reducing the probability of system trespassers manipulating data, and fetching software and data, while on a compromised computer system. Using a similar approach to that described in the aforementioned studies, Jones et al. (2016) deployed the target computers on the Internet infrastructure of a large Chinese university for a period of four months and waited for trespassers to use brute force to access these computers. Once they had accessed the computers, system trespassers were randomly assigned to one of four experimental conditions (i.e. a 2 × 2 factorial design). In the first treatment condition, the target computers were configured to present an 'altruistic' message of moral persuasion. In the second treatment condition, the target computers were set to present a 'standard' legal sanction threat. In the third treatment condition, the target computers were configured to display an 'ambiguous' warning message. Finally, target computers in the control condition were set to present no message to trespassers. The authors found no significant effect from the presence of legal warnings or ambiguous warnings on either the proportion or volume of 'change and fetch' commands entered onto target computers. However, the message of moral persuasion was found to be effective in decreasing both the proportion and volume of 'change and fetch' commands entered by system trespassers on a compromised computer system. Finally, Howell et al. (2017) used the data collected by Jones et al. (2016) to explore the effectiveness of different types of warnings (i.e. sanction threats or moral persuasion) in reducing the probability of 'reconnaissance' commands being entered on the target computers. None of these warnings were found to have a significant effect. These authors speculate that those system trespassers who would have utilised tactical skills to avoid detection on the attacked system were deterred from logging any keystroke command followed by observing the warning.

In summary, warning messages are relatively ineffective in preventing the occurrence of system trespassing events, yet could be somewhat effective in mitigating their consequences and influencing system trespassers' online behaviours in the attacked computer systems. It is worth flagging the one potential limitation of this body of work is that it was not possible to account for automated scripts. It was, therefore, not possible to determine with absolute certainty whether the warning banner was read by a human or merely disrupted the automated script.

One important social configuration that could be incorporated into contemporary computing environments is the implementation of *monitoring and surveillance* in the system (Eivazi 2011; Moore 2000). Indeed, contemporary computer environments can be divided into two broad categories: fortresses and weakly fortified. Fortress computer environments have substantial control and supervision over their users' access to, and operations on, the system (Ciocchetti 2011; Moore 2000), and incorporate security mechanisms that primarily protect against an external attack. Security professionals who maintain these environments perform frequent security audits on these computer networks, and monitor employees' computer and network activities (Hassan et al. 2015). Consistent with the implementation of surveillance in the physical environment (Welsh and Farrington 2009), the application of monitoring in computing environments is intended to increase social control by improving the probability of rapid detection of any undesired use of the system, whether by legitimate (D'Arcy and Herath 2011; Ciocchetti 2011; Moore 2000) or illegitimate users (Hsiao et al. 1979).

Wilson et al. (2015) sought to determine whether a surveillance banner displayed to system trespassers upon entry to a computer system would: (1) reduce the probability of computer commands being entered into the compromised system during the first system trespassing incident; (2) reduce the volume and probability of repeated system trespassing incidents on a target computer; and (3) persist during subsequent system trespassing incidents. These authors deployed target computers on the Internet infrastructure of a large American university for a period of seven months and waited for trespassers to use brute force to access these computers. Once they had accessed the computers, system trespassers were randomly assigned to one of four experimental conditions. In the first condition, the target computers were configured to display a surveillance banner upon each entry to the system. In the second condition, no banner was displayed, yet a surveillance-based process, which could have been easily discovered by the trespassers, was embedded in the background. In the third condition, target computers were configured to present both the surveillance banner and run this surveillance software. In the last condition, the target computers had neither the surveillance banner nor the surveillance software installed. The authors found that the presence of a surveillance banner in the attacked computer system reduced the probability of commands being typed during longer first system trespassing incidents. Further, they reported that the probability of commands being typed during subsequent system trespassing incidents (on the same target computer) was conditioned by the presence of a surveillance banner and by whether commands had been entered during previous trespassing incidents. However, the surveillance banner was found to be ineffective in reducing the volume and probability of repeated system trespassing incidents on a target computer.

FUTURE APPLICATIONS AND ADAPTATIONS TO DIGITAL CONTEXTS

Governmental agencies, private corporations, and individuals around the globe employ a wide range of technical tools and security policies in an effort to reduce their probability of becoming victims of cybercrime. Many of the security tools and procedures coincide with the list of crime prevention strategies that are suggested by the SCP perspective (Homel and Clarke 1997; Cornish and Clarke 2003), which aim to prevent the occurrence of offline crimes.

One key conclusion that can be drawn from this chapter is that rigorous evidence regarding the effectiveness of security tools in preventing and mitigating cybercrime is relatively scarce. Specifically, the available evidence regarding the effectiveness of SCP techniques in preventing cybercrime tends to focus on three key strategies: antivirus products, warnings, and formal surveillance software and tools. Research on the effectiveness of antivirus products in detecting and preventing malware infection reveals that most products are able to detect and prevent most malware attacks. In contrast, research findings from studies that investigate the effectiveness of warning and surveillance in preventing and mitigating malicious hacking reveal that both techniques are limited in their effectiveness to reduce incidents. It remains unknown whether other situational crime preventions techniques, such as firewalls, passwords, and security awareness programs, effectively reduce cybercrime. Given the promise that these strategies carry, we encourage security researchers to empirically assess the effectiveness of these strategies more widely in digital contexts.

One of the underlying reasons behind the relative scarcity of empirical research in this area could be the absence of universally accepted information security frameworks, theories, and measurement metrics to provide organisations with practical tools for assessing the effectiveness of security controls and policies to prevent cybercrime (Torres et al. 2006). Indeed, the most common approach for the implementation of information security practices in governmental and private organisations by Information Technology officers draws on their managers' personal experience in the field and world views (Siponen and Willison 2009). Such an approach does not require rigorous empirical evaluations of security tools and policies in order to support decision-making by these professionals. However, Blakley (2002) suggests that this approach has failed to prevent organisations from becoming the targets and victims of cybercrime. Therefore, Blakely proposes the adoption of an information security approach that monetises information security and calls for quantifying the effectiveness of security tools and policies in achieving their stated goals. Since this approach to information security is still relatively new, there lacks an abundance of evaluations of security control, policies, and tools. However, with time, and with the realisation that organisations should quantify and evaluate both their cyber-related risks and the effectiveness of their security posture in mitigating them, there will likely be an increase in the number of rigorous scientific evolutions of cybersecurity practices in future. Such evaluations should include the development of security metrics that are clear, objective, repeatable, and simple (Atzeni and Lioy 2006). Using such agreed upon metrics (e.g. the volume of malware detected on a computer or the rate of DDoS attacks experienced per day) will allow security experts to improve their organisations' security postures. Moreover, adopting such metrics will facilitate a better understanding of cybercrime displacement both within and between organisations' computer infrastructures. Until then, governmental agencies should support independent and objective scientific efforts that are aimed at testing the effectiveness of security tools and policies in preventing cybercrime, as well as guide practical efforts for facilitating a more secure cyber environment for computer and Internet users around the world.

REFERENCES

Algaith, A., Gashi, I., Sobesto, B., Cukier, M., Haxhijaha, S., & Bajrami, G. (2016, June 28–July 1). Comparing detection capabilities of antivirus products: An empirical study with different versions of products from the same vendors. In *2016 46th Annual IEEE/IFIP International Conference on Dependable Systems and Networks Workshop (DSN-W)* (pp. 48–53). IEEE. https://doi.org/10.1109/DSN-W.2016.45.

Atzeni, A., & Lioy, A. (2006). Why to adopt a security metric? A brief survey. In D. Gollmann, F. Massacci, & A. Yautsiukhin (Eds.), *Quality of protection: Advances in information security* (Vol. 23, pp. 1–12). Boston, MA: Springer. https://doi.org/10.1007/978-0-387-36584-8_1.

AV Comparatives. (2011). *On demand detection of malicious software.* Available at https://www.av-comparatives.org/images/stories/test/ondret/avc_od_feb2011.pdf. Accessed 15 June 2019.

Bace, R., & Mell, P. (2001). *NIST special publication on intrusion detection systems.* Retrieved from the Defense Technical Information Center (ADA393326).

Bell, J., & Burke, B. (1992). *Cruising Cooper Street situational crime prevention: Successful case studies* (2nd ed.). Guilderland, NY: Harrow and Heston.

Bennett, T., Holloway, K., & Farrington, D. P. (2009). A review of the effectiveness of neighbourhood watch. *Security Journal, 22*(2), 143–155. https://doi.org/10.1057/palgrave.sj.8350076.

Berlin, K., Slater, D., & Saxe, J. (2015). Malicious behavior detection using windows audit logs. In *Proceedings of the 8th ACM Workshop on Artificial Intelligence and Security* (pp. 35–44). New York, NY: ACM. https://doi.org/10.1145/2808769.2808773.

Bishop, P., Bloomfield, R., Gashi, I., & Stankovic, V. (2011, November 29–December 2). Diversity for security: A study with off-the-shelf antivirus engines. In *2011 IEEE 22nd International Symposium on Software Reliability Engineering* (pp. 11–19). IEEE. https://doi.org/10.1109/ISSRE.2011.15.

Blais, E., & Bacher, J.-L. (2007). Situational deterrence and claim padding: Results from a randomized field experiment. *Journal of Experimental Criminology, 3*(4), 337–352. https://doi.org/10.1007/s11292-007-9043-z.

Blakley, B. (2002, May 16–17). The measure of information security is dollars. In *Proceedings (online) of the First Annual Workshop on Economics and Information Security (WEIS '02)* (pp. 1–4). Berkeley, CA.

Bonneau, J. (2012, May 20–23). The science of guessing: Analyzing an anonymized corpus of 70 million passwords. In *2012 IEEE Symposium on Security and Privacy* (pp. 538–552). IEEE. https://doi.org/10.1109/SP.2012.49.

Cazier, J. A., & Medlin, B. D. (2006). Password security: An empirical investigation into e-commerce passwords and their crack times. *Information Systems Security, 15*(6), 45–55. https://doi.org/10.1080/10658980601051318.

Ciocchetti, C. A. (2011). The eavesdropping employer: A twenty-first century framework for employee monitoring. *American Business Law Journal, 48*(2), 285–369. https://doi.org/10.1111/j.1744-1714.2011.01116.x.

Clarke, R. V. (1995). Situational crime prevention. *Crime and Justice, 19,* 91–150. https://doi.org/10.1086/449230.

Cornish, D. B., & Clarke, R. V. (2003). Opportunities, precipitators and criminal decisions: A reply to Wortley's critique of situational crime prevention. *Crime Prevention Studies, 16,* 41–96.

Cozens, P. M., Saville, G., & Hillier, D. (2005). Crime prevention through environmental design (CPTED): A review and modern bibliography. *Property Management, 23*(5), 328–356. https://doi.org/10.1108/02637470510631483.

Crawford, A., & Evans, K. (2017). Crime prevention and community safety. In A. Leibling, S. Maruna, & L. McAra (Eds.), *The Oxford handbook of criminology* (6th ed., pp. 797–824). Oxford, UK: Oxford University Press. https://doi.org/10.1093/he/9780198719441.001.0001.

Crow, W. J., & Bull, J. L. (1975) *Robbery deterrence: An applied behavioral science demonstration—Final report.* La Jolla, CA: Western Behavioral Sciences Institute.

Dacey, R. F. (2003). *Information security: Effective patch management is critical to mitigating software vulnerabilities.* Washington, DC: General Accounting Office.

D'Arcy, J., & Herath, T. (2011). A review and analysis of deterrence theory in the IS security literature: Making sense of the disparate findings. *European Journal of Information Systems, 20*(6), 643–658. https://doi.org/10.1057/ejis.2011.23.

Décary-Hétu, D., & Giommoni, L. (2017). Do police crackdowns disrupt drug cryptomarkets? A longitudinal analysis of the effects of Operation Onymous. *Crime, Law and Social Change, 67*(1), 55–75. https://doi.org/10.1007/s10611-016-9644-4.

Eivazi, K. (2011). Computer use monitoring and privacy at work. *Computer Law and Security Review, 27*(5), 516–523. https://doi.org/10.1016/j.clsr.2011.07.003.

Eurostat. (2011). *Nearly one third of internet users in the EU27 caught a computer virus.* Available at https://ec.europa.eu/eurostat/documents/2995521/5028026/4-07022011-AP-EN.PDF/22c742a6-9a3d-456d-bedc-f91deb15481b. Accessed 15 June 2019.

Farrington, D. P. (1993). Understanding and preventing bullying. In M. Tonry (Ed.), *Crime and justice: A review of research* (Vol. 17, pp. 381–458). Chicago, IL: University of Chicago.

Faysel, M. A., & Haque, S. S. (2010). Towards cyber defense: Research in intrusion detection and intrusion prevention systems. *IJCSNS International Journal of Computer Science and Network Security, 10*(7), 316–325.

Florêncio, D., Herley, C., & van Oorschot, P. C. (2016). Pushing on string: The 'don't care' region of password strength. *Communications of the ACM, 59*(11), 66–74. https://doi.org/10.1145/2934663.

Garg, A., Vidyaraman, S., Upadhyaya, S., & Kwiat, K. (2006, April 2–6). USim: A user behavior simulation framework for training and testing IDSes in GUI based systems. In *Proceedings of the 39th Annual Symposium on Simulation (ANSS '06)* (pp. 196–203). Washington, DC: IEEE Computer Society. https://doi.org/10.1109-ANSS.2006.45.

Gerace, T., & Cavusoglu, H. (2009). The critical elements of the patch management process. *Communications of the ACM, 52*(8), 117–121. https://doi.org/10.1145/1536616.1536646.

Guerette, R. T., & Bowers, K. J. (2009). Assessing the extent of crime displacement and diffusion of benefits: A review of situational crime prevention evaluations. *Criminology, 47*(4), 1331–1368. https://doi.org/10.1111/j.1745-9125.2009.00177.x.

Guttman, B., & Roback, E. A. (1995). *An introduction to computer security: The NIST handbook.* Gaithersburg, MD: U.S. Department of Commerce.

Hassan, H. M., Reza, D. M., & Farkhad, M. A.-A. (2015). An experimental study of influential elements on cyberloafing from general deterrence theory perspective case study: Tehran subway organization. *International Business Research, 8*(3), 91. https://doi.org/10.5539/ibr.v8n3p91.

Homel, R., & Clarke, R. (1997). A revised classification of situational crime prevention techniques. In S. P. Lab (Ed.), *Crime prevention at a crossroads* (pp. 17–27). Cincinnati, OH: Anderson.

Howell, C. J., Cochran, J. K., Powers, R. A., Maimon, D., & Jones, H. M. (2017). System trespasser behavior after exposure to warning messages at a Chinese computer network: An examination. *International Journal of Cyber Criminology*, *11*(1). https://doi.org/10.5281/zenodo.495772.

Hsiao, D. K., Kerr, D. S., & Madnick, S. E. (1979). *Computer security*. New York, NY: Academic Press.

Hutchings, A., Clayton, R., & Anderson, R. (2016, June 1–3). Taking down websites to prevent crime. In *2016 APWG Symposium on Electronic Crime Research (eCrime)* (pp. 1–10). https://doi.org/10.1109/ECRIME.2016.7487947.

Hutchings, A., Pastrana, S., & Clayton, R. (2019). Displacing big data: How criminals cheat the system. In E. R. Leukfeldt & T. J. Holt (Eds.), *Cybercrime: The human factor*. Oxon, UK: Routledge.

Jeffrey, C. R., Hunter, R. D., & Griswold, J. (1987). Crime prevention and computer analysis of convenience store robberies in Tallahassee. *Florida Police Journal*, *34*, 65–69.

Jones, H., Maimon, D., & Ren, W. (2016). Sanction threat and friendly persuasion effects on system trespassers' behaviors during a system trespassing event. In T. Holt (Ed.), *Cybercrime through an interdisciplinary lens* (pp. 150–166). London, UK: Routledge. https://doi.org/10.4324/9781315618456.

Kambow, N., & Passi, L. K. (2014). Honeypots: The need of network security. *International Journal of Computer Science and Information Technologies*, *5*(5), 6098–6101.

Korman, M., Välja, M., Björkman, G., Ekstedt, M., Vernotte, A., & Lagerström, R. (2017). Analyzing the effectiveness of attack countermeasures in a SCADA system. In *Proceedings of the 2nd Workshop on Cyber-Physical Security and Resilience in Smart Grids* (pp. 73–78). New York, NY: ACM. https://doi.org/10.1145/3055386.3055393.

Lévesque, F. L., & Fernandez, J. M. (2014, August). *Computer security clinical trials: Lessons learned from a 4-month pilot study*. Paper presented at CSET '14 7th Workshop on Cyber Security Exoerueetation and Test, San Diego, CA.

Lévesque, F. L., Fernandez, J. M., & Batchelder, D., & Young, G. (2016). Are they real? Real-life comparative tests of antivirus products. In *Virus Bulletin Conference* (pp. 1–11).

Lévesque, F., Nsiempba, J., Fernandez, J. M., Chiasson, S., & Somayaji, A. (2013). A clinical study of risk factors related to malware infections. In *Proceedings of the 2013 ACM SIGSAC Conference on Computer & Communications Security* (pp. 97–108). New York, NY: ACM. https://doi.org/10.1145/2508859.2516747.

Lyu, M. R., & Lau, L. K. (2000). Firewall security: Policies, testing and performance evaluation. In *Proceedings 24th Annual International Computer Software and Applications Conference (COMPSAC 2000)* (pp. 116–121). IEEE.

Maimon, D., Alper, M., Sobesto, B., & Cukier, M. (2014). Restrictive deterrent effect of a warning banner in an attacked computer system. *Criminology, 52,* 33–59. https://doi.org/10.1111/1745-9125.12028.

Moore, A. D. (2000). Employee monitoring and computer technology: Evaluative surveillance v. privacy. *Business Ethics Quarterly, 10*(3), 697–709. https://doi.org/10.2307/3857899.

Nayak, K., Marino, D., Efstathopoulos, P., & Dumitraş, T. (2014). Some vulnerabilities are different than others. In A. Stavrou, H. Bos, & C. Portokalidis (Eds.), *Research in Attacks, Intrusions and Defences (RAID 2014)* (LNCS, Vol. 8688, pp. 426–446). Springer. https://doi.org/10.1007/978-3-319-11379-1_21.

PC Security Labs. (2013). *Security solution review on Windows 8 platform.* Technical report. PC Security Labs.

Rama, P., & Kulmala, R. (2000). Effects of variable message signs for slippery road conditions on driving speed and headways. *Transportation Research, 3,* 85–94. https://doi.org/10.1016/S1369-8478(00)00018-8.

Ramsbrock, D., Berthier, R., & Cukier, M. (2007, June 25–28). Profiling attacker behavior following SSH compromises. In *37th Annual IEEE/IFIP International Conference on Dependable Systems and Networks (DSN'07)* (pp. 119–124). IEEE. https://doi.org/10.1109/DSN.2007.76.

Scott, L., Crow, W. J., & Erickson, R. (1985). *Robbery as robbers see it.* Dallas, TX: Southland Corporation.

Seeberg, V. E., & Petrovic, S. (2007). A new classification scheme for anonymization of real data used in IDS benchmarking. In *The Second International Conference on Availability, Reliability and Security (ARES 2007)* (pp. 385–390). IEEE. https://doi.org/10.1109/ARES.2007.9.

Siponen, M., & Willison, R. (2009). Information security management standards: Problems and solutions. *Information & Management, 46*(5), 267–270. https://doi.org/10.1016/j.im.2008.12.007.

Sloan-Howitt, M., & Kelling, G. (1990). Subway graffiti in New York City: 'Getting up' vs. 'meaning' it and 'cleaning' it. *Security Journal, 1*(3), 131–136.

Stockman, M., Heile, R., & Rein, A. (2015). An open-source honeynet system to study system banner message effects on hackers. In *Proceedings of the 4th Annual ACM Conference on Research in Information Technology* (pp. 19–22). New York, NY: ACM. https://doi.org/10.1145/2808062.2808069.

Sukwong, O., Kim, H. S., & Hoe, J. C. (2011). Commercial antivirus software effectiveness: An empirical study. *Computer, 44*(3), 63–70. https://doi.org/10.1109/MC.2010.187.

Surisetty, S., & Kumar, S. (2010). Is McAfee securitycenter/firewall software providing complete security for your computer? In *2010 Fourth International Conference on Digital Society* (pp. 178–181). IEEE.

Testa, A., Maimon, D., Sobesto, B., & Cukier, M. (2017). Illegal roaming and file manipulation on target computers: Assessing the effect of sanction threats on system trespassers' online behaviors. *Criminology and Public Policy, 16*(3), 689–726. https://doi.org/10.1111/1745-9133.12312.

Torres, J. M., Sarriegi, J. M., Santos, J., & Serrano, N. (2006). Managing information systems security: Critical success factors and indicators to measure effectiveness. In S. K. Katsikas, J. López, M. Backes, & S. Gritzalis (Eds.), *Information security: ISC 2006* (Lecture Notes in Computer Science, Vol. 4176, pp. 530–545). Berlin, Germany: Springer. https://doi.org/10.1007/11836810_38.

Welsh, B. C., & Farrington, D. P. (2008a). Effects of closed circuit television surveillance on crime. *Campbell Systematic Reviews, 17*, 2–73. https://doi.org/10.4073/csr.2008.17.

Welsh, B. C., & Farrington, D. P. (2008b). Effects of improved street lighting on crime. *Campbell Systematic Reviews, 13*, 1–51. https://doi.org/10.4073/csr.2008.13.

Welsh, B. C., & Farrington, D. P. (2009). *Making public places safer: Surveillance and crime prevention.* New York, NY: Oxford University Press. https://doi.org/10.1093/acprof:oso/9780195326215.001.0001.

Wilson, T., Maimon, D., Sobesto, B., & Cukier, M. (2015). The effect of a surveillance banner in an attacked computer system: Additional evidence for the relevance of restrictive deterrence in cyberspace. *Journal of Research in Crime and Delinquency, 52*(6), 829–855. https://doi.org/10.1177/0022427815587761.

Wogalter, M. (2006). Purposes and scope of warnings. In M. Wogalter (Ed.), *Handbook of warnings* (pp. 3–10). Boca Raton: CRC Press.

CHAPTER 3

Universal Communication Strategies

Abstract This chapter explores universal communication strategies: mass media messages that aim to deter people from committing crimes. These interventions are underpinned by rational choice theories of crime, and typically attempt to alter individuals' perceptions of the risks and rewards of offending. Mass media communications target a wide audience and have been traditionally applied to common crimes such as drink-driving. We consider the evidence, finding that overall there is very limited support for the effectiveness of communications at reducing offline forms of crime. Though universal communications have been applied to some extent in the digital realm, no evaluations have been conducted to assess their effectiveness. We describe the limitations of such strategies in digital contexts and provide a set of guidelines for design of communication strategies in this realm.

Keywords Advertising · Cyberchoices campaign ·
Mass media campaigns · Mass media messaging ·
Rational choice theory · Universal communications

INTRODUCTION

This chapter examines universal communication strategies, which aim to influence the offender calculus of the risks and rewards of criminal activity. Universal communications are mass media messages primarily

© The Author(s) 2019   35
R. Brewer et al., *Cybercrime Prevention*,
Crime Prevention and Security Management,
https://doi.org/10.1007/978-3-030-31069-1_3

broadcast on television, or through other audio/visual channels (e.g. the Internet), where they can reach a wide audience. Though the content of such messages can vary, typically they aim to deter offenders from considering or committing crimes by warning them about the consequences of engaging in those behaviours. Alternatively, they involve messaging aimed to channel would-be offenders away from crime into alternate behaviour by making this option seem more attractive. A single message might incorporate aspects of both approaches.

In this chapter, we describe the two principal approaches utilised in universal communications, and the theory underlying these approaches. We then critically assess the research evidence for the effectiveness of universal communications. Although universal communications have been widely deployed to reduce the occurrence of common crimes (such as drink-driving and illicit drug use), we find that overall there is very limited support for their effectiveness. Moreover, though universal communications have been applied to some extent in the cyber realm, no empirical research has been conducted to assess whether these interventions have been successful in the online context. We argue that communication campaigns in isolation may be ineffective at shifting behaviour without broader policy and environmental changes that impact the decision landscape. Nevertheless, we provide a set of guidelines for the design of effective communication strategies to prevent cybercrime.

THEORETICAL UNDERPINNINGS OF THE INTERVENTION

Universal communications rely on a number of theories and logic, depending on the content of the particular communication. However, two primary mechanisms underlie the majority of existing communication strategies. First, messages may attempt to change perceptions of the risks of offending. In this common approach, mass media campaigns provide information about the consequences of offending; for example, by threatening punishment (i.e. increasing the perceived risks associated with the behaviour). Judgements of risk are influenced by various aspects, such as the perceived *severity* and *certainty* of the punishment (Nagin 2013; Nagin and Pogarsky 2001). Perceived risks might also be informed by more emotional (Slovic et al. 2004), or psychosocial dimensions, such as perceived social norms (Ajzen 1991; Akers 1990; Bandura 1971)—for example, in advertisement campaigns that try to persuade viewers that antisocial behaviour is 'uncool'. The perceived probability of detection and conviction appears to be the most influential factor in reducing crime (see meta-analysis by Pratt et al. 2008). Therefore, universal communication strategies may be particularly limited when applied to inherently low apprehension crimes (including cybercrime), in which threats of punishment may be perceived as hollow.

The second primary mechanism is to promote *positive* behaviours and values. Such interventions present an alternative to the offending behaviour and associate it with a reward, such that positive ways of responding are reinforced. For example, a communication may present a person who uses streaming websites rather than downloading material illegally as 'cool', boosting the reward associated with the desired behaviour.

Both these mechanisms rely on rational choice models of crime (e.g. Cornish and Clarke 1986; based on classical criminological theory by Beccaria 1764/2009), whereby individuals make broadly rational choices about whether to commit crime or not based on the perceived costs and benefits of engaging in the behaviour.

A special category of universal communications is an appeal to third parties to intervene, though this mechanism is less common. Rather than disclosing information about the crime in order to alert the *offender* as to the risks and rewards of a given behaviour, awareness campaigns may raise *third parties'* awareness of the nature of crime in the hope that they will intervene. For instance, a campaign may educate parents about suspicious behaviours that might suggest their children are engaged in offending behaviour, with the aim of encouraging parents to have a discussion with their children. Essentially, such campaigns appeal to the rewards of intervening (e.g. a personal moral reward for doing the right thing) or to the consequences of not intervening (e.g. a loved one will face penalties).

CURRENT APPLICATIONS

Broadly speaking, universal communications aim to reach as large a proportion of the population as possible, in order to deter individuals before they engage in criminal behaviour. Universal communication strategies are most relevant to individuals without a strong history of engaging in negative behaviours that compete with the desired behaviour change; heavily reinforced behaviours are most difficult to shift. Moreover, once an individual is already entrenched in a criminal lifestyle, a host of additional factors is likely to be maintaining the behaviour

(Laub and Sampson 2001). This makes it increasingly unlikely that a simple media message could be influential.

Appeals to third party intervention, on the other hand, are most likely to function at the secondary or even tertiary prevention level, by alerting third parties to suspicious behaviour so that criminal behaviour is prevented from occurring or reoccurring. Universal communications could also be directed at individuals who are already engaging in criminal activity in order to prevent further escalation (secondary prevention). We explore the utility of more targeted messages aimed at offenders in Chapter 6.

Very little has been done to tackle cybercrime through mass media campaigns, though there have been some attempts to reduce incidences of digital piracy and cryptomarket trade (Adermon and Liang 2014; Bhattacharjee et al. 2006; Ladegaard 2018). Another exception is the UK National Crime Agency's Cyberchoices campaign, a multicomponent cybercrime prevention strategy launched in 2015. In this campaign, a series of short videos were posted online and shown in cinemas emphasising the consequences of cybercrime. Some advertisements showed ex-offenders discussing the way their offending has ruined their lives and promoting legitimate career opportunities for cyber skills, while other advertisements were aimed at parents to raise their awareness of cybercrime. The Cyberchoices strategy also involved design and distribution of in-class teaching materials for school children—though this component is not relevant to this chapter (see instead Chapter 4).

While universal communication strategies are clearly in their infancy in relation to cybercrime, they have been widely deployed in the offline context—albeit selectively. Drink-driving and illicit drug use have been common mass media campaign targets.

Evidence Base for Intervention

We could only identify three studies that have examined the effects of media communications in the cyber context. A quasi-experimental study on digital piracy revealed initial positive gains of publicised anti-piracy laws, but these tended to disappear in the long term when the law was not strongly enforced (Adermon and Liang 2014). A lack of enforcement may reinforce the perception that risk of apprehension is low. Supporting this notion, a survey found that more prolific file sharers had increased awareness of the illegality and sanctions associated with their behaviour, yet were *less* likely to believe they would be caught, relative to low sharers (Cox and Collins 2014).

A potential solution to the problem of low apprehension crimes is to increase the perceived likelihood of detection by publicising successful enforcement activities. One longitudinal study found that legal threats in the USA (in the form of highly publicised lawsuits against file sharers) generally had a negative impact on digital piracy (Bhattacharjee et al. 2006). While the initial public announcement to pursue legal actions against offenders did not necessarily reduce piracy (in fact, some increased their file sharing), the news of lawsuits being filed against offenders decreased piracy, particularly after more intrusive measures were employed to track down offenders. In contrast, Ladegaard (2018) failed to find a positive effect of law enforcement media coverage on cybercrime. Using a time series analysis, this study examined the effects of media coverage of cryptomarket arrests and related law enforcement efforts on digital drug trade activity. In fact, trade *increased* after periods with elevated media coverage, and also after court events. Analysis of cryptomarket forum discussions following these events suggested that subjective perceptions of risk may be harder to budge, or less effective in deterring criminal activity, when such behaviour is ideologically driven (i.e. morally justified by perpetrators). Moreover, discussions revealed that the prosecution of a drug market founder was perceived to be a result of chance (specifically, an amateur mistake that could have been avoided), such that publicised prosecutions may inadvertently betray weaknesses in law enforcement systems and thereby reduce the perceived risk of apprehension (Ladegaard 2018).

While evidence of the effectiveness of universal communications in reducing cybercrime are limited at this time, there is a wealth of evidence regarding universal communication strategies in the offline context. Overall, universal communications have had very mixed success at reducing reoffending, though campaigns vary considerably in terms of their content and thus their effects. There is an incredibly large number of ways that such a strategy could be deployed (i.e. variance in the specific characteristics of the message). Beyond this there is a diverse range of individual and situational factors varying across crime contexts that may influence the effectiveness of a particular strategy at any one time. Nevertheless, some of the broad research findings are highlighted below.

As will be detailed across a range of behaviours, the most effective media strategies for behaviour change have typically consisted of more than a one-off communication about the consequences of a behaviour—they must also provide a solution. When individuals are not presented with an adequate means to change their behaviour, fear can motivate avoidance (Rogers 1975; Witte and Allen 2000). Moreover, when threat appeals are too strong, emotional response may interfere with message processing (Petty and Wegener 1998). It is not surprising, then, that health campaigns that rely on fear alone are ineffective. For instance, a quasi-experimental study found that homosexual men reacted to the AIDS 'grim reaper' campaign in Australia the 1980s with helplessness and avoidance of behaviour change, relative to those receiving sensitive, sexually positive material or no material at all (Rosser 1992).

Two recent meta-analyses found that mass media campaigns in isolation had no effect or a negative effect (i.e. an *increase*) on young peoples' illicit drug use (Ferri et al. 2013; Werb et al. 2011). Werb et al. (2011) caution that anti-drug campaigns can increase curiosity and the perception that drug use is widespread, leading to increased drug use. These iatrogenic effects appear to be more marked for younger teen audiences. A survey examining the impact of an anti-drug campaign in the USA revealed that campaign awareness was associated with increased drug use for 12–14 year olds but not for 15–18 year olds (Scheier and Grenard 2010). Additionally, another meta-analysis indicated that media efforts to reduce substance abuse are most effective when messages include alternatives to use and positive attitudes towards *non*-use (Derzon and Lipsey 2002).

It is difficult, however, to separate the effect of media campaigns from the policy changes that often accompany them (Wakefield et al. 2010). Intensive mass media campaigns have been shown to have some effect on reducing smoking initiation in young people (Brinn et al. 2010; Wakefield et al. 2010), but changes in tobacco pricing, availability, and advertising over the same time period have likely all played a role in the decreased prevalence of smoking. Indeed, scholars argue that the most effective programs focusing on alcohol use tend to include broader policy-driven environmental changes (Kelly-Weeder et al. 2011). Similarly, media campaigns can be effective in reducing drink-driving rates across the whole population when they are accompanied by *visible enforcement* (i.e. increasing the certainty of detection; Elder et al. 2004; Tay 2005;

Wakefield et al. 2010). This is consistent with research in Australia which found that random breath testing was more effective than legislation (i.e. punishment certainty was more important than punishment severity), thus the most effective threats must be highly publicised, enforced, and difficult to evade (Homel 1990). This is, of course, a challenging task for crimes that are difficult to police, as noted earlier in the chapter regarding efforts to reduce digital piracy and drug market trade.

It is worth noting that much of the research showing positive effects of communication strategies on drink-driving is not specific to a particular age group. Nevertheless, some research suggests that younger audiences might be more resistant to such communications, and may in fact respond negatively to such messages, with some expressing an increased intention to drink-drive (Glendon and Cernecca 2003; but note that this was on a self-report measure of behavioural *intention*, not commission). Glendon and Cernecca suggest that their findings might be explained by reactance (Brehm 1966), whereby individuals' motivation to engage in a behaviour increases when their freedom to engage in that behaviour is threatened. The desire for independence and individuality, along with a disavowal of authority, is common in adolescence (Hong et al. 1994). The potential for reactance in this group is, therefore, relatively high. Reactance may be particularly problematic for crimes where the threatened behaviour is greatly valued by the person.

It may also be difficult to deter crimes that are characterised by strong rewards that virtually supersede any potential risks. A dated—but relatively robust study—evaluated a television campaign designed to deter vandalism by young boys in England in 1978. The campaign ran two advertisements: one showed a young boy being visited by a police officer (i.e. increasing the perceived severity and/or risk of apprehension); and the other was aimed at parents, imploring them to more closely supervise their children. Despite this two-pronged approach, the campaign was unsuccessful at reducing rates of vandalism in a quasi-experimental trial across several districts (Riley and Mayhew 1980). In explaining the failure of the campaign, Riley and Mayhew expressed scepticism about the ability of mass media to counteract the strong social forces which underlie and immediately precede vandalism offences. For young people in particular, crime can confer social acceptance and status in delinquent peer groups (Warr 2002). This may explain why delinquent peers is one of the most consistent predictors of criminal recidivism in young people (Cottle et al. 2001; Grieger and Hosser 2014; Lipsey and Derzon 1998;

McGrath and Thompson 2012; Simourd and Andrews 1994). Thus, the more one is surrounded by criminal peers who model criminal behaviour, provide rewards for criminal behaviour, and inflict punishment for failing to engage in criminal behaviour (i.e. social rejection), the less influential external threats of punishment will be (Matthews and Agnew 2008).

If crime prevention agencies do not understand their target audience, they have little chance at designing an effective educational strategy. Researchers in the health field (where communication strategies have a long history) have emphasised that media campaigns must use researched and tailored messaging that is appropriate to the audience (Brinn et al. 2010). Importantly, universal communications have been most effective when health campaigns understand their target audience—their motivations for engaging in the negative behaviour and the elements most likely to persuade that audience—and provide useful concrete solutions and information about how to overcome barriers to desired behaviour (see systematic reviews by Everett et al. 2011; Grilli et al. 2002; Noar et al. 2009; Vidanapathirana et al. 2005). Young people in particular might respond well to messages high in sensation value and when they come from credible spokespeople (Derzon and Lipsey 2002).

Due to some of the problems in influencing offenders' behaviour directly, a number of communication strategies have instead chosen to appeal to third parties. The most notable example of this is the Crime Stoppers program, which airs details of a crime on television (often accompanied by video footage of the suspect) and asks members of the public to come forward with information. Evaluations have concluded that Crime Stoppers schemes in general are effective in the detection and prosecution of crime, though these evaluations did not use comparison groups or other quality evaluation methodologies (Gresham et al. 2001; Rosenbaum et al. 1989). While it is difficult to know whether such crimes would have been otherwise solved, some commentators are confident that these appeals can be useful (Challinger 2004). However, note that Riley and Mayhew's (1980) more robust study of the anti-vandalism campaign discussed above, in which parents were alerted to the possibility that their children were committing vandalism, did not increase parental supervision or reduce crime rates. Third party intervention strategies rely on two conditions: that third parties are aware of the crime and the identity of the criminal (difficult for more covert criminal activities); and that third parties are willing and able to intervene in an effective manner. In the above case, parents may have been unwilling to sanction their children in a meaningful way that reduced vandalism. The nature of the intervention demanded from third parties will thus influence its success. It is important to make realistic and feasible demands of third parties.

Future Applications and Adaptations to Digital Contexts

While there is no research that can speak to the effectiveness of universal communications in reducing cybercrime, the nature of Internet connectivity and policing strategies to affect cybercrime in particular demonstrate that it is extremely difficult to influence the offender calculus. The benefits of cybercrime can be substantial, and the risk of detection seems low, making it difficult to deter offenders. Furthermore, the fact that (potential) offenders can readily displace from one target to another in the face of either sophisticated detection techniques or security makes it exceedingly difficult to influence their decision to desist completely.

Furthermore, peer associations may diminish the perceived value of strategies, as they may be able to shape vicarious perceptions of the certainty of punishment. For young people who have very strong online peer networks and environmental features that promote criminal behaviour, it could be hard to develop effective deterrence messaging even if salience and severity of the threat is quite high. Moreover, campaigns might inadvertently increase the perceived value of criminal activities via reactance or curiosity. Focusing solely on the negative outcomes of engaging in cybercrime, especially if the message is seen as illegitimate by adolescents (e.g. delivered by police) is likely to have limited effectiveness in preventing cybercrime.

Interventions that condemn negative online behaviour while also promoting positive behaviours or attitudes may have some success if used early on. Successful adoption of desired behaviours will rely on repeated reinforcement, which would require highly saturated, long-term media campaigns. Moreover, the content of the message will be critical to its success and relies on detailed knowledge of the target audience (cyber-offenders). Research has not yet reliably established the psychological and social profiles of cyber-offenders, far less their perceptions of the costs and benefits of cybercrime (i.e. obstacles to desistance and incentives for change). Without such knowledge, it would be difficult to pitch a media message appropriately and formulate potential positive behaviours in this space. Strategies to resist peer pressure may be one potential element of such interventions, given the role of peers in cyber-crime (Bossler and Burruss 2011; Holt et al. 2012; Skinner and Fream 1997). In any case, communication strategies would be better used as a part of a wider approach and should not be expected to deliver substantial behaviour change alone.

Appeals to third parties may have limited reach. Cybercrime can be committed privately and with relative anonymity, thus there may be a very small pool of potential third party targets for intervention who are aware of the offending behaviour. From a parent's perspective, it may be particularly difficult to distinguish potential cybercrime activity from innocuous online behaviour (i.e. spending time on the Internet). It is also unclear what the message should be, if any. Parents may be unlikely to report their children to the police, but they may benefit from some softer advice (e.g. to have a discussion with their children about cybercrime).

References

Adermon, A., & Liang, C.-Y. (2014). Piracy and music sales: The effects of an anti-piracy law. *Journal of Economic Behavior & Organization, 105*, 90–106. https://doi.org/10.1016/j.jebo.2014.04.026.

Ajzen, I. (1991). The theory of planned behavior. *Organizational Behavior and Human Decision Processes, 50*, 179–211. https://doi.org/10.1016/0749-5978(91)90020-T.

Akers, R. L. (1990). Rational choice, deterrence, and social learning theory in criminology: The path not taken. *The Journal of Criminal Law and Criminology, 81*, 653–676.

Bandura, A. (1971). *Social learning theory.* New York, NY: General Learning.

Beccaria, C. (2009). *On crimes and punishments* (G. R. Newman & P. Marongiu, Trans.). New Brunswick, NJ: Transaction Publishers (Original work published 1764).

Bhattacharjee, S., Gopal, R. D., Lertwachara, K., & Marsden, J. R. (2006). Impact of legal threats on online music sharing activity: An analysis of music industry legal actions. *The Journal of Law and Economics, 49*, 91–114. https://doi.org/10.1086/501085.

Bossler, A. M., & Burruss, G. W. (2011). The general theory of crime and computer hacking: Low self-control hackers? In T. J. Holt & B. H. Schell (Eds.), *Corporate hacking and technology-driven crime: Social dynamics and implications* (pp. 38–67). Hershey, PA: IGI Global. https://doi.org/10.4018/978-1-61692-805-6.ch003.

Brehm, J. W. (1966). *A theory of psychological reactance.* New York, NY: Academic.

Brinn, M. P., Carson, K. V., Esterman, A. J., Change, A. B., & Smith, B. J. (2010). Mass media interventions for preventing smoking in young people. *Cochrane Database of Systematic Reviews, 11.* https://doi.org/10.1002/14651858.CD001006.pub2.

Challinger, D. (2004). *Crime stoppers Victoria: An evaluation.* Canberra, Australia: Australian Institute of Criminology.

Cornish, D. B., & Clarke, R. V. (1986). Rational choice approaches to crime. In D. B. Cornish & R. V. G. Clarke (Eds.), *The reasoning criminal: Rational choice perspectives on offending* (pp. 1–16). New York, NY: Springer-Verlag.

Cottle, C. C., Lee, R. J., & Heilbrun, K. (2001). The prediction of criminal recidivism in juveniles: A meta-analysis. *Criminal Justice and Behavior, 28,* 367–394. https://doi.org/10.1177/0093854801028003005.

Cox, J., & Collins, A. (2014). Sailing in the same ship? Differences in factors motivating piracy of music and movie content. *Journal of Behavioral and Experimental Economics, 50,* 70–76. https://doi.org/10.1016/j.socec.2014.02.010.

Derzon, J. H., & Lipsey, M. W. (2002). A meta-analysis of the effectiveness of mass-communication for changing substance-use knowledge, attitudes, and behavior. In W. D. Crano & M. Burgoon (Eds.), *Mass media and drug prevention: Classic and contemporary theories and research* (pp. 231–258). Mahwah, NJ: Lawrence Erlbaum. https://doi.org/10.4324/9781410603845-11.

Elder, R. W., Shults, R. A., Sleet, D. A., Nichols, J. L., Thompson, R. S., & Rajab, W. (2004). Effectiveness of mass media campaigns for reducing drinking and driving and alcohol-involved crashes: A systematic review. *American Journal of Preventive Medicine, 27,* 57–65. https://doi.org/10.1016/j.amepre.2004.03.002.

Everett, T., Bryant, A., Griffin, M. F., Martin-Hirsch, P. P., Forbes, C. A., & Jepson, R. G. (2011). Interventions targeted at women to encourage the uptake of cervical screening. *Cochrane Database of Systematic Reviews, 5.* https://doi.org/10.1002/14651858.CD002834.pub2.

Ferri, M., Allara, E., Bo, A., Gasparrini, A., & Faggiano, F. (2013). Media campaigns for the prevention of illicit drug use in young people. *Cochrane Database of Systematic Reviews, 6.* https://doi.org/10.1002/14651858.CD009287.pub2.

Glendon, A. I., & Cernecca, L. (2003). Young drivers' responses to anti-speeding and anti-drink-driving messages. *Transportation Research Part F: Traffic Psychology and Behaviour, 6,* 197–216. https://doi.org/10.1016/S1369-8478(03)00026-3.

Gresham, P., Stockdale, J., Bartholomew, I., & Bullock, K. (2001). *An evaluation of the impact of Crimestoppers.* London, UK: Home Office.

Grieger, L., & Hosser, D. (2014). Which risk factors are really predictive? An analysis of Andrews and Bonta's "Central Eight" risk factors for recidivism in

German youth correctional facility inmates. *Criminal Justice and Behavior, 41,* 613–634. https://doi.org/10.1177/0093854813511432.

Grilli, R., Ramsay, C., & Minozzi, S. (2002). Mass media interventions: Effects on health services utilisation. *Cochrane Database of Systematic Reviews, 1.* https://doi.org/10.1002/14651858.CD000389.

Holt, T. J., Bossler, A. M., & May, D. C. (2012). Low self-control, deviant peer associations, and juvenile cyberdeviance. *American Journal of Criminal Justice, 37,* 378–395. https://doi.org/10.1007/s12103-011-9117-3.

Homel, R. (1990). Random breath testing and random stopping programs in Australia. In R. J. Wilson & R. E. Mann (Eds.), *Drinking and driving: Advances in research and prevention* (pp. 159–202). New York, NY: Guilford.

Hong, S.-M., Giannakopoulos, E., Laing, D., & Williams, N. A. (1994). Psychological reactance: Effects of age and gender. *The Journal of Social Psychology, 134,* 223–228. https://doi.org/10.1080/00224545.1994.9711385.

Kelly-Weeder, S., Phillips, K., & Rounseville, S. (2011). Effectiveness of public health programs for decreasing alcohol consumption. *Patient Intelligence, 3,* 29–38. https://doi.org/10.2147/PI.S12431.

Ladegaard, I. (2018). We know where you are, what you are doing and we will catch you: Testing deterrence theory in digital drug markets. *The British Journal of Criminology, 58*(2), 414–433. https://doi.org/10.1093/bjc/azx021.

Laub, J. H., & Sampson, R. J. (2001). Understanding desistance from crime. *Crime and Justice, 28,* 1–69. https://doi.org/10.1086/652208.

Lipsey, M. W., & Derzon, J. H. (1998). Predictors of violent or serious delinquency in adolescence and early adulthood: A synthesis of longitudinal research. In R. Loeber & D. P. Farrington (Eds.), *Serious and violent offenders: Risk factors and successful interventions* (pp. 86–105). Thousand Oaks, CA: Sage. https://doi.org/10.4135/9781452243740.n6.

Matthews, S. K., & Agnew, R. (2008). Extending deterrence theory: Do delinquent peers condition the relationship between perceptions of getting caught and offending? *Journal of Research in Crime and Delinquency, 45,* 91–118. https://doi.org/10.1177/0022427807313702.

McGrath, A., & Thompson, A. P. (2012). The relative predictive validity of the static and dynamic domain scores in risk-need assessment of juvenile offenders. *Criminal Justice and Behavior, 39,* 250–263. https://doi.org/10.1177/0093854811431917.

Nagin, D. S. (2013). Deterrence: A review of the evidence by a criminologist for economists. *Annual Review of Economics, 5,* 83–105. https://doi.org/10.1146/annurev-economics-072412-131310.

Nagin, D. S., & Pogarsky, G. (2001). Integrating celerity, impulsivity, and extralegal sanction threats into a model of general deterrence: Theory and evidence. *Criminology, 39,* 865–892. https://doi.org/10.1111/j.1745-9125.2001.tb00943.x.

Noar, S. M., Palmgreen, P., Chabot, M., Dobransky, N., & Zimmerman, R. S. (2009). A 10-year systematic review of HIV/AIDS mass communication campaigns: Have we made progress? *Journal of Health Communication, 14,* 15–42. https://doi.org/10.1080/10810730802592239.

Petty, R. E., & Wegener, D. T. (1998). Attitude change: Multiple roles for persuasion variables. In D. T. Gilbert, S. T. Fiske, & G. Lindzey (Eds.), *The handbook of social psychology* (pp. 323–390). Boston, MA: McGraw-Hill.

Pratt, T. C., Cullen, F. T., Blevins, K. R., Daigle, L. E., & Madensen, T. D. (2008). The empirical status of deterrence theory: A meta-analysis. In F. T. Cullen, J. P. Wright, & K. R. Blevins (Eds.), *Taking stock: The status of criminological theory* (pp. 367–396). New Brunswick, NJ: Transaction Publishers. https://doi.org/10.4324/9781315130620-14.

Riley, D., & Mayhew, P. (1980). *Crime prevention publicity.* London, UK: Home Office.

Rogers, R. W. (1975). A protection motivation theory of fear appeals and attitude change. *Journal of Psychology, 91,* 93–114. https://doi.org/10.1080/00223980.1975.9915803.

Rosenbaum, D. P., Lurigio, A. J., & Lavrakas, P. J. (1989). Enhancing citizenship participation and solving serious crime: A national evaluation of Crime Stoppers programs. *Crime and Deliquency, 35,* 401–420. https://doi.org/10.1177/0011128789035003006.

Rosser, B. S. (1992). The effects of using fear in public AIDS education on the behaviour of homosexually active men. *Journal of Psychology and Human Sexuality, 4,* 123–134. https://doi.org/10.1300/J056v04n03_09.

Scheier, L. M., & Grenard, J. L. (2010). Influence of a nationwide social marketing campaign on adolescent drug use. *Journal of Health Communication, 15,* 240–271. https://doi.org/10.1080/10810731003686580.

Simourd, L., & Andrews, D. A. (1994). Correlates of delinquency: A look at gender differences. *Forum on Corrections Research, 6,* 26–31.

Skinner, W. F., & Fream, A. M. (1997). A social learning theory analysis of computer crime among college students. *Journal of Research in Crime and Delinquency, 34,* 495–518. https://doi.org/10.1177/0022427897034004005.

Slovic, P., Finucane, M. L., Peters, E., & MacGregor, D. G. (2004). Risk as analysis and risk as feelings: Some thoughts about affect, reason, risk, and rationality. *Risk Analysis, 24*(2), 311–322. https://doi.org/10.1111/j.0272-4332.2004.00433.x.

Tay, R. (2005). Mass media campaigns reduce the incidence of drinking and driving. *Evidence-Based Healthcare and Public Health, 9,* 26–29. https://doi.org/10.1016/j.ehbc.2004.11.013.

Vidanapathirana, J., Abramson, M. J., Forbes, A., & Fairley, C. (2005). Mass media interventions for promoting HIV testing. *Cochrane Database of Systematic Reviews, 3.* https://doi.org/10.1002/14651858.CD004775.pub2.

Wakefield, M. A., Loken, B., & Hornik, R. C. (2010). Use of mass media campaigns to change health behaviour. *The Lancet, 376*(9748), 1261–1271. https://doi.org/10.1016/S0140-6736(10)60809-4.

Warr, M. (2002). *Companions in crime: The social aspects of criminal conduct.* New York, NY: Cambridge University Press. https://doi.org/10.1017/cbo9780511803956.

Werb, D., Mills, E. J., DeBeck, K., Kerr, T., Montaner, J. S., & Wood, E. (2011). The effectiveness of anti-illicit-drug public-service announcements: A systematic review and meta-analysis. *Journal of Epidemiology and Community Health, 65,* 834–840. https://doi.org/10.1136/jech.2010.125195.

Witte, K., & Allen, M. (2000). A meta-analysis of fear appeals: Implications for effective public health campaigns. *Health Education and Behavior, 27,* 591–615. https://doi.org/10.1177/109019810002700506.

PART II

Secondary Forms of Prevention

CHAPTER 4

Educational Workshops

Abstract This chapter investigates the use of educational workshops in preventing crime. This type of intervention brings together groups of individuals deemed at risk of offending to educate them about the consequences of crime, or to promote positive behaviours and skills that reduce the likelihood of committing crime. Though educational workshops vary widely in terms of theory and content, most commonly they rely on social-cognitive theories of learning. School-based workshops have been applied extensively to combat illicit drug use, gang involvement, and general delinquency with varying success—some with positive effects, and some with negative effects. We conclude that workshops can be an effective way to reduce crime, but this depends greatly on the content and style of workshop deployed. However, to date, this strategy has not been widely utilised to deal with cybercrime; consequently, there is virtually no research on the success (or otherwise) of this strategy. We discuss the applicability of workshops in this space, explicating the features that would likely increase the success of this intervention in reducing cybercrime.

Keywords Cyberbullying · Educational workshops · Skill building · Social learning theory

© The Author(s) 2019
R. Brewer et al., *Cybercrime Prevention*,
Crime Prevention and Security Management,
https://doi.org/10.1007/978-3-030-31069-1_4

INTRODUCTION

This chapter explores the use of educational workshops in preventing online and offline crimes. This intervention brings together groups of (potential) offenders in single or multiple sessions for the purposes of educating them about the nature of crime, and reinforcing prosocial values and behaviours. Typically, programs are deployed within school curricula, or may selectively target at-risk adolescents. Workshops can be didactic (i.e. a presentation of information), but as will be argued, the active ingredient in workshop effectiveness is the inclusion of interactive elements, such as discussion, role-play, and providing practical strategies to combat antisocial behaviour. Specialised programming using trained professionals has also been used to reduce problematic behaviour, but this tends to be high cost (requiring clinicians to work directly with families and/or schools, as well as individuals) and intensive (e.g. Hay et al. 2015; Goorden et al. 2016). In this chapter, we instead examine generic workshops that can be easily and broadly implemented.

This chapter first outlines the theoretical underpinnings for this type of intervention, describing the various features of workshops that are thought to reduce crime. We then summarise the evidence for this type of intervention in the offline context, as well as potential pitfalls. We conclude that workshops can be an effective way to reduce crime, but this depends greatly on the content and style of workshop deployed. Finally, we discuss the applicability of workshops to prevent cybercrime, explicating the features that would likely increase the success of this intervention in the online space.

THEORETICAL UNDERPINNINGS OF THE INTERVENTION

Though educational workshops vary widely in terms of theory and content, most commonly they rely on social-cognitive theories of learning. That is, criminal behaviour is understood as a learned behaviour that is the result of both social and personal factors (Ajzen 1991; Akers 1990; Bandura 1971). Workshops focus on providing information about the negative consequences of crime, as well as teaching psychosocial skills, such as peer refusal, decision-making, and interpersonal communication. Particular attention is often paid to resisting negative peer influences, as the presence of delinquent peers represents one of the most well-established risk factors for offending (Bonta and Andrews 2017).

Experiential and interactive components of workshops (e.g. role playing and practicing skills) are thought to be critical in reinforcing desired behaviours and cementing prosocial habits (e.g. Gneezy et al. 2011).

Current Applications

The majority of programming is aimed at young adults, with some targeting youth under the age of 10 years. The bulk is focused at youth in primary or secondary schools to affect early onset offending behaviours. Others more explicitly target groups or individuals deemed to be at risk of offending, for example workshops for pre-delinquents (those attracting disciplinary action at school but not yet committing serious offences). As a result, it can be argued that workshops are meant to affect youth during the onset or potential acceleration phase of offending, constituting both primary and secondary modes of crime prevention.

We were able to identify only a few instances of workshops that specifically target cybercrime. For example, the UK's National Crime Agency, in partnership with the Cyber Security Challenge UK, released a lesson plan for teachers to educate pupils about the nature and effects of cybercrime. Workshops identified through published research articles, however, tended to focus on protecting victims from possible harm (rather than targeting potential offenders). In contrast, workshops have been—and are—widely deployed in the offline context, most commonly to target illicit drug use, involvement in gangs, and general delinquency, as well as broader health behaviours.

Evidence Base for Intervention

To date, there is minimal empirical research on the application of workshops to cybercrime. One of the few peer-reviewed studies published in this space reviewed existing cyber psychoeducation programs for children (Mishna et al. 2009). Most of these were aimed at preventing online victimisation, but some targeted perpetration of problematic online behaviours. Of particular relevance is the i-SAFE program—a classroom-based curriculum containing five lessons (lasting approximately 40 minutes each), which provides children with information about potential hazards on the Internet, approaches for safely dealing with those hazards, and activities to help them think about the knowledge they receive and share with their peers. Chibnall et al. (2006) conducted a quasi-experimental evaluation of i-SAFE across 18 schools in the USA for children aged 9–14 years old. Results showed that over a nine-month period, the program had some success in changing attitudes and knowledge behaviour (e.g. knowledge of intellectual property and piracy), but it had minimal impact on changing offender behaviours (e.g. spending time on inappropriate websites). Though the authors speculated that this failure was due to low baseline rates of the behaviours studied, other reasons may also be offered. The program was delivered offline, and while it had an active learning approach (asking students to think about their own behaviour and talk with each other to develop perspectives and solutions), in practice teachers reported that 'time constraints forced them to use lecture rather than activities to teach the curriculum (Chibnall et al. 2006, p. 36). Thus, the learning was in fact rather abstract and didactic, and there were few opportunities to practice or reinforce actual positive online behaviours within the workshop sessions. Without experiential and interactive activities, workshops are likely to be very limited in their effects on behaviour change (Botvin and Griffin 2004; Soole et al. 2008; Tobler and Stratton 1997).

Studies on cyberbullying are also potentially informative here, as the phenomenon operates under similar dynamics to cybercrime, including a lack of supervision, high accessibility of opportunities for negative behaviours in the online environment, and perceived social anonymity. Best practice for targeting cyberbullying tends to use comprehensive, whole-of-school interventions (e.g. Pearce et al. 2011), but we located two studies that examined the effectiveness of discrete workshop-based programs in preventing the perpetration of cyberbullying. Both studies showed favourable results for the intervention.

The first: the Arizona Attorney General's Social Networking Safety Promotion and Cyberbullying Prevention (SNSPCP) presentation, is a school-based, single-session workshop for middle school (10–15-year old) students. The presentation works on three levels, attempting to: (a) change students' attitudes, intentions, and behaviours, (b) convince students that personally relevant and serious threats exist, and (c) provide students with effective techniques to reduce the threats that they are able to perform. The presentation was evaluated using a trial with random allocation to treatment (presentation) or control (no presentation). Despite its short exposure—a single session—there were significant effects on self-reported attitudes towards safe Internet use, perception of the certainty of punishment for cyberbullying, and behavioural intentions to cyberbully others (Roberto et al. 2014). However, no measures of actual behaviour change were assessed.

Another program developed in Germany, Media Heroes, consists of a set of modules run by teachers over either 10 sessions or a one-day intensive workshop. It has three components: raising awareness of the consequences and legal risks of cyberbullying; changing norms (e.g. increasing social responsibility through moral reasoning exercises); and empathy training (using perspective-taking exercises). It also offers strategies to protect oneself from becoming victimised. An evaluation (also using random allocation) of a group of 11–17-year-old students found that the program reduced self-reported aggressive behaviour and perpetrated cyberbullying at nine months follow up, with slightly stronger effects indicated for the multisession format (Wölfer et al. 2014). Both the Media Heroes and SNSPCP programs were experimental designs, providing a good degree of reliability for the findings. Overall, workshops for cyberbullying appear very promising.

Moving away from online deviance, there is a body of evidence we can draw upon in understanding the effects of educational workshops in reducing crime in general. Overall, the evidence suggests that workshops can be an effective way to change behaviour, but there is variance depending on the type and mode of program implemented. For instance, systematic reviews have found that school-based workshops that are interactive, challenge beliefs and norms, and develop problem solving and coping skills, can: reduce illicit substance use (Agabio et al. 2015); violent behaviour (Park-Higgerson et al. 2008; Wilson and Lipsey 2008); and general delinquency (Wilson et al. 2001). Similarly, sex education workshops that address risk and protective factors for (unsafe) sexual practices in a psychologically safe environment by focusing on building positive skills rather than imbuing fear have also been effective (Kirby et al. 2007). Too many individual programs exist to detail every single one; the results of the reviews above provide sufficient evidence that this type of intervention has utility in reducing criminal behaviour. We will now discuss the effects of some of the most popular and well-researched programs, particularly those providing important lessons regarding the potential effectiveness of such strategies in the cyber context.

One of the more widely disseminated workshop programs targeting early adolescents is the Life Skills Training (LST) program developed in the USA, designed to reduce drug and alcohol use as well as general delinquent behaviour. LST is an intensive program that involves 30 sessions taught over a three year period (15 sessions in the first year, 10 in the second year, and five in the third year) with additional modules for violence prevention in each year. Training is typically delivered in class by regular teachers and is designed to enhance personal self-management skills, as well as social skills to overcome feelings of shyness, engage with peers in effective ways, and respond to social challenges using verbal and non-verbal skills. The program also emphasises the development of resistance skills to combat peer pressure. The program has been found to be successful in the reduction of juvenile drug and alcohol use (Botvin and Griffin 2004). The studies are robust, using random assignment to the experimental and control groups, and diverse sample populations.

An additional model of note is the recent Promoting School-University Partnerships to Enhance Resilience (PROSPER) intervention (Osgood et al. 2013). It is not a program proper, but a delivery system focused on implementing treatment programs efficiently and effectively through university, school, and community partnerships. It also evaluates their outcomes. An example of this strategy in action was implemented to affect negative peer influence through a reduction in the individual network centrality of antisocial students in broader social networks (Osgood et al. 2013). It focused on the implementation of existing substance use programming—including the Strengthening Families Program, Life Skills Training Program, All Stars Program, and Project Alert—tracking the network centrality and influence of prosocial students relative to antisocial students in school communities. Using 28 rural and semi-rural school districts in Iowa ($n = 14$) and Pennsylvania ($n = 14$) based on matched characteristics, a sample of students in grade six were targeted through a family-focused intervention followed by a school-based intervention during seventh grade (Osgood et al. 2013). The students were then followed through grade nine to assess the utility of the treatment. The findings demonstrated that the treatment reduced the influence of antisocial youth in friendship networks relative to control (e.g. Osgood et al. 2013, 2015). Evidence also suggests that the program is associated with reduced illicit substance use and conduct problems (Spoth et al. 2011).

Other popular programs have limited evidence of effectiveness. Programming like the G.R.E.A.T. program (developed by law enforcement agencies in the USA) has a specific component related to the formation of prosocial peers, prosocial activity involvement, bonding with non-delinquent peers, and higher bonding with police. The initial implementation of the program, involving nine one-hour lessons administered over a nine-week period, was linked with short-term reports of lower rates of victimisation, negative views of gangs, and greater associations with prosocial peers (Esbensen and Osgood 1999). A later, more robust randomised study (following a substantial revision to the program) found that the program promoted positive attitudes and behaviours, and reduced gang membership at one year and four years post treatment (Esbensen et al. 2013). However, effects on associations with delinquent peers, violent offending, and general delinquency were non-significant in both the one- and four-year periods. As a result, G.R.E.A.T. appears to have a generally small effect on crime over the long term.

There have been a number of documented cases of workshops producing negative effects—that is, increasing the likelihood of criminal activity. One of the most infamous examples is Scared Straight program, which was rolled out in schools across the USA through the 1980s and 1990s with much enthusiasm. Aiming to scare children from committing crime, the program involved visits to prisons where at-risk juveniles were given confrontational presentations by inmates about life in prison. Unfortunately, scholars have since concluded that the program increased the odds of criminal behaviour (see review by Petrosino et al. 2013). The mechanism underlying the increase in crime is unclear, but one hypothesis is that placing troubled youth together and allowing them to interact can reinforce problem behaviour—a process of peer contagion (Cho et al. 2005; Dishion et al. 1999; Rhule 2005). Group programming also introduces the danger that antisocial youth might victimise prosocial youth in the group (Zhao et al. 2016).

Similarly, a meta-analytic review of a popular school-based program for children, Drug Abuse Resistance Education (DARE), found that it had little to no effect on illicit drug use, and in some cases increased drug use (West and O'Neal 2004). There are two possible reasons for this. First, DARE is didactic, instructing children about the effects and consequences of drug use. The program could have simply piqued young peoples' interest in drugs without building personal and social skills that might promote non-use (see also Sanchez et al. 2017). A second explanation for the findings points to the key role played by program facilitators. DARE is delivered by police officers—towards whom young people can feel disinterest or animosity. An authoritarian atmosphere, coupled with a didactic educational style, is unlikely to promote an inclusive and interactive learning environment, which is critical in facilitating behaviour change (Rosenbaum and Hanson 1998). It should also be noted that the G.R.E.A.T. program (which was inspired by DARE) is primarily delivered by uniformed law enforcement officers. This same explanation might also account for G.R.E.A.T.'s limited effects.

FUTURE APPLICATIONS AND ADAPTATIONS TO DIGITAL CONTEXTS

As already noted, there has been some application of educational workshops in the cyber realm with promising results—at least for cyberbullying. However, more empirical work is needed to evaluate high-quality programming before a firm conclusion can be drawn regarding the utility of such interventions in this space. Successful adoption of desired behaviours will rely on repeated reinforcement, which would require multisession interactive workshops.

Certainly, there are some reasons to be optimistic about the potential for such programming. The literature on cybercrime offending has highlighted the significant role of social learning in online criminality (Bossler and Burruss 2011; Holt et al. 2012; Skinner and Fream 1997). Given this, peer and social influence elements of workshop programming may have some impact on cybercrime. The difficulty in this programming lies in the notion that individuals' online social networks would need to be targeted just as heavily as those in the offline world. Strategies to resist online peer pressures would need to be a key element of such interventions. However, there is no clear research to date as to how to effectively communicate such information, aside from existing programs regarding risks of victimisation from talking to strangers online. Such an issue requires substantive investigation in order to determine the efficacy of any program.

Workshops may also need to recognise and communicate the inherent fallacies of the techniques of neutralisation espoused by cyber-offenders (e.g. Chua and Holt 2016; Morris 2011; Turgeman-Goldschmidt 2008). It would be essential to minimise the acceptance of criminal norms associated with hacking (e.g. websites or computers with open vulnerabilities do not deserve to be exploited). This may be effective, but would have to be implemented in early childhood so as to capture youth before an interest in technology could take root.

Lastly, extreme caution should be taken in implementing workshops with at-risk youth; that is, where group members hold antisocial attitudes that could be transmitted to lower-risk group members. Best practice in these cases involves using highly structured programming and careful monitoring (e.g. Hektner et al. 2017).

References

Agabio, R., Trincas, G., Floris, F., Mura, G., Sancassiani, F., & Angermeyer, M. C. (2015). A systematic review of school-based alcohol and other drug prevention programs. *Clinical Practice and Epidemiology in Mental Health, 11,* 102–112. https://doi.org/10.1111/j.1465-3362.2012.00517.x.

Ajzen, I. (1991). The theory of planned behavior. *Organizational Behavior and Human Decision Processes, 50,* 179–211. https://doi.org/10.1016/0749-5978(91)90020-T.

Akers, R. L. (1990). Rational choice, deterrence, and social learning theory in criminology: The path not taken. *The Journal of Criminal Law and Criminology, 81,* 653–676.

Bandura, A. (1971). *Social learning theory.* New York, NY: General Learning.

Bonta, J., & Andrews, D. A. (2017). *The psychology of criminal conduct* (6th ed.). New York, NY: Routledge.

Bossler, A. M., & Burruss, G. W. (2011). The general theory of crime and computer hacking: Low self-control hackers? In T. J. Holt & B. H. Schell (Eds.), *Corporate hacking and technology-driven crime: Social dynamics and implications* (pp. 38–67). Hershey, PA: IGI Global. https://doi.org/10.4018/9781616928056.ch003.

Botvin, G. J., & Griffin, K. W. (2004). Life skills training: Empirical findings and future directions. *The Journal of Primary Prevention, 25*(2), 211–232. https://doi.org/10.1023/B:JOPP.0000042391.58573.5b.

Chibnall, S., Wallace, M., Leicht, C., & Lunghofer, L. (2006). *I-SAFE evaluation: Final report.* Fairfax, VA: Caliber.

Cho, H., Hallfors, D., & Sanchez, V. (2005). Evaluation of a high school peer group intervention for at risk youth. *Journal of Abnormal Child Psychology, 33,* 363–374. https://doi.org/10.1007/s10802-005-3574-4.

Chua, Y. T., & Holt, T. J. (2016). A cross-national examination for the techniques of neutralization to account for hacking behaviors. *Victims and Offenders, 11,* 534–555. https://doi.org/10.1080/15564886.2015.1121944.

Dishion, T. J., McCord, J., & Poulin, F. (1999). When interventions harm: Peer groups and problem behavior. *American Psychologist, 54,* 755–764. https://doi.org/10.1037/0003-066X.54.9.755.

Esbensen, F. A., & Osgood, D. W. (1999). Gang resistance education and training (GREAT): Results from a national evaluation. *Journal of Research in Crime and Delinquency, 36*, 194–225. https://doi.org/10.1177/00224278 99036002004.

Esbensen, F. A., Osgood, D. W., Peterson, D., Taylor, T. J., & Carson, D. C. (2013). Short- and long-term outcome results from a multisite evaluation of the G.R.E.A.T. Program. *Criminology and Public Policy, 12*, 375–411. https://doi.org/10.1111/1745-9133.12048.

Gneezy, U., Meier, S., & Rey-Biel, P. (2011). When and why incentives (don't) work to modify behavior. *The Journal of Economic Perspectives, 25*, 191–209. https://doi.org/10.1257/jep.25.4.191.

Goorden, M., van der Schee, E., Hendricks, V. M., & Hakkaart-van Roijen, L. (2016). Cost-effectiveness of multidimensional family therapy compared to cognitive behavioural therapy for adolescents with a cannabis use disorder: Data from a randomized controlled trial. *Drug and Alcohol Dependence, 162*, 154–161. https://doi.org/10.1016/j.drugalcdep.2016.03.004.

Hay, C., Wang, X., Ciaravolo, E., & Meldrum, R. C. (2015). Inside the black box: Identifying the variables that mediate the effects of an experimental intervention for adolescents. *Crime and Delinquency, 61*, 243–270. https://doi.org/10.1177/0011128711398030.

Hektner, J. M., Brennan, A. L., & August, G. J. (2017). Incorporating well-adjusted peers in a conduct problems prevention program: Evaluation of acceptability, fidelity, and safety of implementation. *School Mental Health, 9*, 66–77. https://doi.org/10.1007/s12310-016-9199-7.

Holt, T. J., Bossler, A. M., & May, D. C. (2012). Low self-control, deviant peer associations, and juvenile cyberdeviance. *American Journal of Criminal Justice, 37*, 378–395. https://doi.org/10.1007/s12103-011-9117-3.

Kirby, D. B., Laris, B., & Rolleri, L. A. (2007). Sex and HIV education programs: Their impact on sexual behaviors of young people throughout the world. *Journal of Adolescent Health, 403*, 206–217. https://doi.org/10.1016/j.jadohealth.2006.11.143.

Mishna, F., Cook, C., Saini, M., Wu, M.-J., & MacFadden, R. (2009). Interventions for children, youth, and parents to prevent and reduce cyber abuse. *Campbell Systematic Reviews, 2*. https://doi.org/10.4073/csr.2009.2.

Morris, R. G. (2011). Computer hacking and the techniques of neutralization: An empirical assessment. In T. J. Holt & B. H. Schell (Eds.), *Corporate hacking and technology-driven crime: Social dynamics and implications* (pp. 1–17). Hershey, PA: IGI Global. https://doi.org/10.4018/9781616928056.ch001.

Osgood, D. W., Feinberg, M. E., Gest, S. D., Moody, J., Ragan, D. T., Spoth, R., et al. (2013). Effects of PROSPER on the influence potential of prosocial versus antisocial youth in adolescent friendship networks.

Journal of Adolescent Health, 53, 174–179. https://doi.org/10.1016/j. jadohealth.2013.02.013.

Osgood, D. W., Feinberg, M. E., & Ragan, D. T. (2015). Social networks and the diffusion of adolescent problem behavior: Reliable estimates of selection and influence from sixth through ninth grades. *Prevention Science, 16,* 832–843. https://doi.org/10.1007/s11121-015-0558-7.

Park-Higgerson, H. K., Perumean-Chaney, S. E., Bartolucci, A. A., Grimley, D. M., & Singh, K. P. (2008). The evaluation of school-based violence prevention programs: A meta-analysis. *Journal of School Health, 78*(9), 465–479. https://doi.org/10.1111/j.1746-1561.2008.00332.x.

Pearce, N., Cross, D., Monks, H., Waters, S., & Falconer, S. (2011). Current evidence of best practice in whole-school bullying intervention and its potential to inform cyberbullying interventions. *Australian Journal of Guidance and Counselling, 21,* 1–21. https://doi.org/10.1375/ajgc.21.1.1.

Petrosino, A., Turpin-Petrosino, C., Hollis-Peel, M. E., & Lavenberg, J. G. (2013). 'Scared Straight' and other juvenile awareness programs for preventing juvenile delinquency. *Campbell Systematic Reviews, 5.* https://doi.org/10.4073/csr.2013.5.

Rhule, D. M. (2005). Take care to do no harm: Harmful interventions for youth problem behavior. *Professional Psychology: Research and Practice, 36,* 618–625. https://doi.org/10.1037/0735-7028.36.6.618.

Roberto, A. J., Eden, J., Savage, M. W., Ramos-Salazar, L., & Deiss, D. M. (2014). Outcome evaluation results of school-based cybersafety promotion and cyberbullying intervention for middle school students. *Health Communication, 29,* 1029–1042. https://doi.org/10.1080/10410236.2013.831684.

Rosenbaum, D. P., & Hanson, G. S. (1998). Assessing the effects of school-based drug education: A six-year multilevel analysis of project D.A.R.E. *Journal of Research in Crime and Delinquency, 35,* 381–412. https://doi.org/10.1177/0022427898035004002.

Sanchez, Z. M., Valente, J. Y., Sanudo, A., Pereira, A. P. D., Cruz, J. I., Schneider, D., et al. (2017). The #Tamojunto drug prevention program in Brazilian schools: A randomized controlled trial. *Prevention Science, 18*(7), 772–782. https://doi.org/10.1007/s11121-017-0770-8.

Skinner, W. F., & Fream, A. M. (1997). A social learning theory analysis of computer crime among college students. *Journal of Research in Crime and Delinquency, 34,* 495–518. https://doi.org/10.1177/0022427897034004005.

Soole, D. W., Mazerolle, L., & Rombouts, S. (2008). School-based drug prevention programs: A review of what works. *Australian and New Zealand Journal of Criminology, 41*(2), 259–286. https://doi.org/10.1375/acri.41.2.259.

Spoth, R., Redmond, C., Clair, S., Shin, C., Greenberg, M., & Feinberg, M. (2011). Preventing substance misuse through community–university partnerships: Randomized controlled trial outcomes 4½ years past baseline. *American*

Journal of Preventive Medicine, 40, 440–447. https://doi.org/10.1016/j. amepre.2010.12.012.

Tobler, N. S., & Stratton, H. H. (1997). Effectiveness of school-based drug prevention programs: A meta-analysis of the research. *Journal of Primary Prevention, 18,* 71–128. https://doi.org/10.1023/A:1024630205999.

Turgeman-Goldschmidt, O. (2008). Meanings that hackers assign to their being a hacker. *International Journal of Cyber Criminology, 2,* 382.

West, S. L., & O'Neal, K. K. (2004). Project D.A.R.E. outcome effectiveness revisited. *American Journal of Public Health, 94,* 1027–1029. https://doi. org/10.2105/ajph.94.6.1027.

Wilson, D. B., Gottfredson, D. C., & Najaka, S. S. (2001). School-based prevention of problem behaviors: A meta-analysis. *Journal of Quantitative Criminology, 17*(3), 247–272. https://doi.org/10.1023/A:1011050217296.

Wilson, S. J., & Lipsey, M. W. (2008). School-based interventions for aggressive and disruptive behavior: Update of a meta-analysis. *American Journal of Preventative Medicine, 33*(2), S130–S143. https://doi.org/10.1016/j. amepre.2007.04.011.

Wölfer, R., Schultze-Krumbholz, A., Zagorscak, P., Jäkel, A., Göbel, K., & Scheithauer, H. (2014). Prevention 2.0: Targeting cyberbullying @ school. *Prevention Science, 15,* 879–887. https://doi.org/10.1007/s11121-013-0438-y.

Zhao, S., Chen, X., Ellis, W., & Zarbatany, L. (2016). Affiliation with socially withdrawn groups and children's social and psychological adjustment. *Journal of Abnormal Child Psychology, 44,* 1279–1290. https://doi.org/10.1007/s10802-015-0120-x.

CHAPTER 5

Mentoring Programs

Abstract This chapter examines interventions that can be broadly categorised as mentoring. Mentoring is underpinned by a philosophy that promotes supportive interpersonal relationships that offer guidance to young people throughout their social-emotional, cognitive, and identity development. This chapter chronicles the popularity of mentoring as being one of the most commonly deployed interventions to prevent youth delinquency across traditional contexts, while at the same time drawing together a robust evaluation research literature that reveals only a modest-moderate effect associated with the intervention for those at risk of, or already engaged in, delinquency. Although to date, no research has examined either the utility or efficacy of mentoring as an intervention to target young people involved in cybercrime, we nevertheless argue that key lessons can be drawn from the extant offline crime prevention literature about future prospects in digital contexts. In making these arguments, we tease out the various factors associated with successful mentoring interventions and create a blueprint for the future design and deployment of such interventions.

Keywords Cognitive development · Identity development · Juvenile delinquency · Mentoring programs · Social-emotional development

© The Author(s) 2019
R. Brewer et al., *Cybercrime Prevention*,
Crime Prevention and Security Management,
https://doi.org/10.1007/978-3-030-31069-1_5

Introduction

This chapter examines the utility and efficacy of mentoring programs as an intervention, which broadly defined, involve the 'commitment of time and specific efforts by a more experienced person to the development of mutually beneficial, supportive and nurturing relationship with a less experienced person' (Moodie and Fisher 2009, p. 1). Programs incorporating such supportive relationships are regarded as having utility as a *corrective* experience and intervention for at-risk youth who have experienced poor relations with parents or other caregivers (Grossman et al. 2012) and are designed to enhance the personal development of affected young people (Ainsworth 1989; Rhodes 2005). More precise definitions as to what mentoring interventions entail vary across contexts and with respect to outcomes (e.g. reducing forms of delinquency and/ or aggression, promoting scholastic achievement and/or better health outcomes, etc.).

To begin, this chapter probes the theoretical footings on which assumptions about the utility of mentoring are based. It then chronicles the popularity of this intervention as being one of the most commonly deployed to prevent youth delinquency across traditional crime prevention contexts, while at the same time drawing together a robust evaluative research literature that reveals only a modest-moderate effect associated with the intervention for those at risk of, or already engaged in, delinquency. Although to date no research has examined either the utility or efficacy of mentoring as an intervention to target young people involved in cybercrime, we nevertheless argue that key lessons can be drawn from the extant research literature about future prospects in digital contexts. In making these arguments, we tease out the various factors associated with successful mentoring interventions and create a blueprint for the future design and deployment of such interventions.

Theoretical Underpinnings of the Intervention

Mentoring interventions are rooted in a wider body of research that stresses the importance and enduring prosocial benefits of having positive and supportive interpersonal relationships that offer guidance to children and adolescents throughout their development (Magnusson and Stattin 2006; Scales et al. 2006). More specifically, Rhodes (2002, 2005) argues that establishing and promoting such positive interpersonal foundations serve to mobilise interacting developmental processes across three areas. The first involves *social-emotional development*, whereby the provision and modelling of supportive and caring relationships can serve to challenge negative views held by young people of themselves, peers, and other adults (Hayes et al. 1996). Moreover, the act of both listening to and modelling effective mature communication strategies can play a role in helping young people better understand, regulate, cope with, and express their emotions (McDowell et al. 2002). Second, supportive interpersonal relationships can also serve as a vehicle through which learning can occur socially and promote *cognitive development*. Research has found that young people can, through collaborative learning experiences, develop new lateral thinking skills, and appreciation for prosocial values, norms, and perspectives (Radziszewska and Rogoff 1991; Vygotsky 1978). Third, mentoring relationships can also play a role in shifting youth perceptions of their current and future selves and thereby promote *identity development* (DuBois et al. 2011). Such development can inform choices made about how to behave. Indeed, Darling et al. (2002) argue that substantial interpersonal relationships with mentors have scope to introduce young people to new activities and resources, as well as educational and vocational opportunities, which they can draw upon to develop their identities over time.

In order to attain these developmental objectives, mentoring interventions seek to support close positive relationships between young people and (typically) adult volunteers. Mentoring interventions are increasingly commonplace and take shape through various community-based and school or site-based programs. The scope of these programs is broad and encompasses a diverse range of outcomes that focus on an assortment of not only delinquent behaviours (including drug and alcohol use, among other antisocial activities), but scholastic (e.g. academic performance, drop-outs) and health-related (e.g. obesity) issues as well. Given the wide applicability of potential mentoring interventions to areas tangential to crime prevention, only specifically stated delinquency-related outcomes (e.g. reported offending by self or others, as well as arrest and juvenile court records) are considered in this chapter. However, we acknowledge the important links between low educational performance, certain physiological conditions, poor health, and delinquency.

CURRENT APPLICATIONS

The targets for relevant mentoring interventions generally include those young people who either exhibit a previous or current history of delinquent behaviour or exhibit certain characteristics that are assessed as at risk for juvenile delinquency. The precise definition of what characteristics are captured by the 'at risk' label in this context can vary from intervention to intervention. They tend to correspond to a host of individual and environmental risk factors that have been shown to increase the likelihood of delinquency in later adolescence and adulthood (Tolan 2002; Tolan et al. 2013). Individual risk factors include evidence of elevated levels of aggression, conduct disorders, and poor academic performance, as well as antisocial attitudes, beliefs, and values. Environmental risk factors, on the other hand, include social and familial factors, such as place of residence; socio-economic status; family and parental influences (particularly the conviction/incarceration of family members); exposure to violence, abuse, and gangs; and negative peer relations and influences (Matz 2014; Tolan and Gorman-Smith 2003).

Although there is scant reference to the use of mentoring interventions in digital contexts, such interventions targeting at-risk populations have been deployed across numerous offline contexts at various stages of the offending life cycle. Interventions targeting at-risk youth are abundant and oriented towards *prevention*, with a focus on reducing the likelihood of the onset of offending. Interventions targeting juvenile offenders are also commonplace—with their focus being either *diversionary* or *treatment* oriented—addressing the acceleration phase of offending or promoting desistance.

Mentoring interventions represent one of the most commonly deployed interventions with respect to the prevention, diversion, and remediation of youth involved in, or at risk of, delinquent behaviour (Tolan et al. 2013). Within offline contexts, the popularity of such interventions has seen considerable investment in, and deployment across, the world. Such deployment has principally been through the use of an extensive variety of community-based programs, as well as school or site-based programs. Some programs are highly localised in nature (confined to a particular school, community or district), while other larger initiatives operate at state, national, and in some cases—including the oft-cited and researched Big Brothers Big Sisters program—operate on a global scale.

The remit for these programs is broad and tends to involve young people who are referred as a preventative measure and as a consequence of presenting as being at-risk. Moreover, mentoring interventions have also been applied in a treatment capacity in cases where young people have a demonstrated history of prior offending behaviour. However, in such cases, there is considerable variation as to the inclusion or intake criteria of specific mentoring programs. These range from including only young people with limited exposure to formal criminal proceedings (i.e. police cautions, but no formal charges brought), to involving those with more robust histories that include prior convictions for a wide variety of offences, such as substance use (drugs and alcohol), motor vehicle theft, burglary, criminal mischief, disorderly conduct and assault (Blechman et al. 2000; Fo and O'Donnell 1975; Hanlon et al. 2002).

EVIDENCE BASE FOR THE INTERVENTION

While at present, no publicly available peer-reviewed evaluation research has examined either the utility or efficacy of mentoring as an intervention to target young people involved in cybercrime, considerable scholarly attention has evaluated the use of such interventions in an offline context. That is, there exists a substantial body of experimental and quasi-experimental research that has evaluated the links between mentoring and delinquency across a multiplicity of contexts, involving specific programs within certain regions, and with specific mentee and mentor characteristics. The resultant available evidence reporting specifically on the effectiveness of such interventions on delinquency outcomes have produced somewhat mixed results.

Some evaluations of mentoring interventions have reported very promising results. For example, Tierney et al.'s (1995) highly cited impact study of the Big Brothers Big Sisters mentoring program—involving 10–16-year-olds over an 18-month period—utilised a random assignment experimental design and found that participants were less likely to start using drugs/alcohol, less likely to hit others, and experienced improved educational outcomes and peer relationships after partaking in the program. Along these same lines, Keating et al.'s (2002) non-experimental study of an intensive mentoring program involving youth (10–17 years old) at risk for juvenile delinquency or mental illness in the Western USA found that mentoring had a broad positive influence, particularly with respect to the escalation of emotional and behavioural problems that include delinquency. Elsewhere, in their study of similarly aged youth, Fo and O'Donnell (1975) used a random assignment experimental design to find that the community-based buddy system offered significant benefit with respect to reducing the likelihood of delinquency during the project year for both those with prior offending histories (i.e. marked desistance) and those without (i.e. prevention of onset). More recently, Hanlon et al.'s (2002) random assignment experimental study of mentoring groups (as opposed to one-on-one relationships) in inner-city Baltimore found a significant impact upon delinquent (including violent) behaviour during the one year follow-up period. Elsewhere, Barnes et al.'s (2017) quasi-experimental study of school-based violence also found that mentoring was associated with lower prevalence of student bullying and verbal abuse towards teachers.

On the other hand, there is also mounting evidence that mentoring interventions do not work as intended with respect to delinquency outcomes (Matz 2014). In a random assignment experimental study of the US Department of Education's Student Mentoring Program, Berstein et al. (2009) reported no statistically significant impacts on students who were at risk for, or engaging in, delinquent behaviour (self-reported or school-reported). Blechman et al.'s (2000) non-experimental study of juvenile offenders concluded that mentored youth were more likely to recidivate than those involved in either skill/vocational training or other standard juvenile-diversion programs. Elsewhere, Royse's (1998) random assignment experimental evaluation of the four year Brothers Project also found no evidence of impact from mentoring upon delinquency among 14–16-year-old African Americans. Berger and Gold's (1978) random assignment experimental study also found that volunteer mentoring programs (including voluntary probation and volunteer group counselling) had a negligible effect on reducing a probationer's delinquent behaviour, and that some participating in a volunteer tutoring program actually increased participation in delinquent behaviour.

In recent years, a number of systematic reviews and rapid evidence assessments, focusing largely on experimental and quasi-experimental studies, have sought to reconcile these disparate findings (e.g. Lipsey and Wilson 1998; DuBois et al. 2002, 2011; Jolliffe and Farrington 2007; Tolan et al. 2013). This work has generally concluded that mentoring interventions '*may* [emphasis added] be valuable for those at risk or already involved in delinquency and for associated outcomes' (Tolan et al. 2013, p. 4). In fact, Tolan et al.'s (2013, p. 29) most recent review specifically parses out evaluations that list delinquency and drug use as outcomes and observe a modest positive effect of mentoring interventions. In drawing such conclusions, the reviewers note factors impacting positive outcomes:

- *Relationship attributes:* significantly larger effects were observed when emotional support and advocacy were emphasised in the relationship (Tolan et al. 2013).
- *The mentor's motivation for being a mentor:* effects were larger when professional development and career advancement was an explicit motive for mentor participation (Tolan et al. 2013).
- *Frequency and duration of interactions:* mentoring relationships that were more frequent (i.e. more than once a week) and longer in duration were associated with a reduction in recidivism (Jolliffe and Farrington 2007).
- *Coupling with other interventions:* mentoring proved most successful in reducing recidivism when supplemented by other interventions, and was not as effective when used as the only intervention (Jolliffe and Farrington 2007; Tolan et al. 2013).

Similar conclusions were also drawn by those specific studies that both supported and contested the efficacy of mentoring with respect to delinquent outcomes:

- *Qualities of the mentor:* effectiveness is tied to the quality of training provided to mentors (Herrera et al. 2007; also see Dubois et al. 2011). Mentors who are adults (as opposed to peers) and have prior in-common experiences with mentees are the most influential in achieving positive behavioural change (Ware 2013).
- *Mentoring approach:* mentoring is unlikely to produce change where the mentor is authoritarian or judgemental, where there is too much emphasis on expected behavioural change (rather than building a friendship first), and when too many goals are set, causing the mentee to become discouraged and give up (Ware 2013).

It is also worth noting that numerous studies cite the positive benefits associated with the *total length of the intervention.* However, there lacks universal agreement as to its effect. For example, Jolliffe and Farrington (2007) found that longer mentoring programs did not present as being more effective than shorter interventions (also see Keating et al. 2002; Royse 1998). They believe that this was most likely associated with the difficulty in recruiting high-quality mentors over long periods of time. However, as Chan et al. (2013, pp. 130–131) found, 'mentees who experienced longer relationships and relationships of higher quality ... derived more benefits than those in shorter or lower quality relationships' (see also Herrera et al. 2007; Tierney et al. 1995). This point is further supported by Ware (2013) who argues that long-term mentoring relationships of at least 12–18-month duration, that are based on common interests, mutual respect, genuine friendship, and a fun, non-judgemental approach, have a positive effect on delinquency outcomes.

When all this evidence is considered together, the take-home message about mentoring as an intervention is positive (even from studies that question its impact on delinquency). For example, Blechman et al. (2000, pp. 153–154) suggest that 'when mentoring happens in a natural, uncontrived fashion, and when mentoring involves a one-on-one relationship with a protégé, there is good reason to believe that the mentor-protege relationship serves as a pivotal turning point in the life of a high-risk youth'. Moreover, despite its relatively small effect size, scholars acknowledge that the explosive growth of mentoring interventions, and thus the high volume of youths mentored through such programs, can ultimately produce beneficial and cost-effective outcomes for a large number of young people (Rhodes 2008).

One important caveat stressed by Tolan et al. (2013), as well as others (i.e. DuBois et al. 2011; Rhodes 2008), about the meta-reviews and individual studies canvassed, is that most of the evaluative data available for comparison offers incomplete information with respect to other moderating factors of mentoring intervention effects. For example, most of the studies fail to provide clarity around whether or not mentoring is the sole intervention or if it is used in concert with other preventive or intervention strategies. Many also fail to report the frequency of contact between mentor and mentee, the nature of activities undertaken, as well as the total duration of those relationships. Further information pertaining to mentee characteristics were often omitted, including details of their interpersonal histories and social competencies (DuBois et al. 2002, 2011). Additionally, little information was also made available with respect to the level of training provided to mentors, as well as their assessment and evaluation. Without this knowledge, it is difficult to ascertain whether the positive outcomes reported were as a direct result of the mentoring intervention applied.

We, therefore, stress the importance of considering the above results with caution. On this point, Pawson (2004, p. 2) provides valuable insight, suggesting that the available evidence does not yield a 'thumbs up or thumbs down' for mentoring, but only 'circumstantial and conditional truths'. He contends that available evidence illustrates that relationships cannot be forced and sometimes take the path of least resistance with the most disaffected youths going un-mentored. As such, mentoring does not always go where it is most needed, and while mentors often have wisdom, they do not always have the resources to create and sustain major and long-term changes. Close relationships—even ones voluntarily and willingly tendered—cannot, in isolation, necessarily sweep away the institutional and structural forces that impact a young person's life.

FUTURE APPLICATIONS AND ADAPTATIONS TO DIGITAL CONTEXTS

While there currently exists a dearth of available literature exploring the applicability of mentoring to cyber-dependent crimes, further examination is warranted given the underlying theoretical premise (social-emotional, cognitive, and identity development) and potential benefits of the intervention for reducing the likelihood of delinquency. As alluded to in Chapter 1, a growing body of empirical work has flagged the important role of social interaction and the learning associated with an enhanced capacity to engage in criminal undertakings (Bossler and Burruss 2011; Holt et al. 2012; Skinner and Fream 1997). In particular, recent research emphasises the agency of personal, private, and intimate offline relationships for cyber-offenders, particularly with respect to sustaining interest and developing new skills (Holt 2009; Meyer 1989; Schell and Dodge 2002; Steinmetz 2015). It is, therefore, possible that the timely establishment of a mentoring relationship between a young person and a mentor could have utility, and warrants exploratory study.

It is worth noting that mentoring, as it is currently situated, is likely to yield the most benefit through its application as a diversionary or treatment intervention, as opposed to one oriented towards prevention for at-risk youth. This is because the various criteria or risk factors used to identify at-risk youth would need to be developed and tested to cater towards this unique target population. While only little is known about the offender profiles of cyber-offenders, it is clear from the available evidence that such individuals are likely to exhibit different ecological and individual risk factors than those involved in other forms of delinquency. For example, unlike the poor educational and employment outcomes noted in the above commentary, research shows that malicious cyber-offenders often demonstrate comparably high levels of achievement in both areas (Bachmann 2010; Holt 2007; Schell and Dodge 2002; Weulen Kranenbarg et al. 2019). While some scholars have noted that some malicious cyber-offenders do have histories of familial or adjustment problems (Holt and Schell 2013), these outcomes are not necessarily linked to routine exposure to violence, abuse, drug and alcohol use, or having incarcerated parents. Elsewhere, scholars have noted that cyber-offenders are more likely to exhibit certain behavioural traits including narcissism, anxiety, and depression (Schell and Dodge 2002), as well as lack of empathy and ethical flexibility (Holt and Schell 2013), while other behavioural traits, including elevated levels of aggression, do not appear to be as prevalent.

This point, coupled with the relative scarcity of individuals who ultimately develop the technical wherewithal and desire to hack, could make it difficult to develop a sufficiently targeted list for this population. Accordingly, interventions targeting young people already identified as participating in cybercrimes may be better suited as a first step forward. Such individuals can potentially be identified through a variety of means including parent, teacher, and counsellor referrals, as well as those made by police or courts where available. Such targeting would also be consistent with best practice models put forward by some other evaluators who suggest that mentoring interventions are potentially most effective when applied to those individuals who have come into contact with the police (Jolliffe and Farrington 2007).

Given the importance the mentoring literature places upon the qualities of the mentor and the social dynamics of the relationship with respect to attaining positive outcomes, it is also necessary to consider the practical matter of building a pool of suitable mentors. Willing volunteers with interest or experience in computers and cybersecurity, alongside pertinent social skills, may prove to be in short supply and difficult to recruit (particularly outside of urban areas).

REFERENCES

Ainsworth, M. D. S. (1989). Attachments beyond infancy. *American Psychologist*, *44*, 709–716. https://doi.org/10.1037/0003-066X.44.4.709.

Bachmann, M. (2010). The risk propensity and rationality of computer hackers. *The International Journal of Cyber Criminology*, *4*, 643–656.

Barnes, T. N., Leite, W., & Smith, S. W. (2017). A quasi-experimental analysis of schoolwide violence prevention programs. *Journal of School Violence, 16*(1), 49–67. https://doi.org/10.1080/15388220.2015.1112806.

Berger, R. J., & Gold, M. (1978). An evaluation of a juvenile court volunteer program. *Journal of Community Psychology, 6,* 328–333. https://doi.org/10.1002/1520-6629(197810)6:4<328:AID-JCOP2290060409>3.0.CO;2-K.

Berstein, L., Rappaport, C., Olsho, L., Hunt, D., & Levin, M. (2009). *Impact evaluation of the US Department of Education's student mentoring program* (NCEE 2009–4047).

Blechman, E., Maurice, A., Buecker, B., & Helberg, C. (2000). Can mentoring or skill-training reduce recidivism? Observational study with propensity analysis. *Prevention Science, 1,* 139–155. https://doi.org/10.1023/A:1010073222476.

Bossler, A. M., & Burruss, G. W. (2011). The general theory of crime and computer Hacking: Low self-control hackers? In T. J. Holt & B. H. Schell (Eds.), *Corporate hacking and technology-driven crime: Social dynamics and implications* (pp. 38–67). Hershey, PA: IGI Global. https://doi.org/10.4018/9781616928056.ch003.

Chan, C., Rhodes, J., Howard, W., Lowe, S., Schwartz, S., & Herrera, C. (2013). Pathways of influence in school-based mentoring: The mediating role of parent-teacher relationships. *Journal of School Psychology, 51,* 129–142. https://doi.org/10.1016/j.jsp.2012.10.001.

Darling, N., Hamilton, S., Toyokawa, T., & Matsuda, S. (2002). Naturally occurring mentoring in Japan and the United States: Roles and correlates. *American Journal of Community Psychology, 30,* 245–270. https://doi.org/10.1023/A:1014684928461.

DuBois, D., Holloway, B., Valentine, J., & Cooper, H. (2002). Effectiveness of mentoring programs for youth: A meta-analytic review. *American Journal of Community Psychology, 30,* 157–197. https://doi.org/10.1023/A:1014628810714.

DuBois, D., Portillo, N., Rhodes, J., Silverthorn, S., & Valentine, J. (2011). How effective are mentoring programs for youth? A systematic assessment of the evidence. *Psychological Science in the Public Interest, 12,* 57–91. https://doi.org/10.1177/1529100611414806.

Fo, S. O., & O'Donnell, C. R. (1975). The buddy system: Effect of community intervention on delinquent offenses. *Behavior Therapy, 6,* 522–524. https://doi.org/10.1016/S0005-7894(75)80008-6.

Grossman, J. B., Chan, C. S., Schwartz, S. E. O., & Rhodes, J. E. (2012). The test of time in school-based mentoring: The role of relationship duration and re-matching on academic outcomes. *American Journal of Community Psychology, 49,* 43–54. https://doi.org/10.1007/s10464-011-9435-0.

Hanlon, T., Bateman, R., Simon, B., O'Grady, K., & Carswell, S. (2002). An early community-based intervention for the prevention of substance abuse and other delinquent behaviour. *Journal of Youth and Adolescence, 31,* 459–471. https://doi.org/10.1023/A:1020215204844.

Hayes, A. H., Castonguay, L. G., & Goldfried, M. R. (1996). Effectiveness of targeting the vulnerability factors of depression in cognitive therapy. *Journal of Consulting and Clinical Psychology, 64,* 623–627. https://doi.org/10.1037/0022-006X.64.3.623.

Herrera, C., Grossman, J. B., Kauh, T. J., Feldman, A. F., McMaken, J., & Jucovy, L. Z. (2007). *Making a difference in schools: The Big Brothers Big Sisters school-based mentoring impact study.* Philadelphia, PA: Public/ Private Ventures.

Holt, T. J. (2007). Subcultural evolution? Examining the influence of on- and off-line experiences on deviant subcultures. *Deviant Behavior, 28,* 171–198. https://doi.org/10.1080/01639620601131065.

Holt, T. J. (2009). Lone hacks or group cracks: Examining the social organization of computer hackers. In F. Schmalleger & M. Pittaro (Eds.), *Crimes of the Internet* (pp. 336–355). Upper Saddle River, NJ: Pearson Prentice Hall.

Holt, T. J., Bossler, A. M., & May, D. C. (2012). Low self-control, deviant peer associations, and juvenile cyberdeviance. *American Journal of Criminal Justice, 37,* 378–395. https://doi.org/10.1007/s12103-011-9117-3.

Holt, T. J., & Schell, B. H. (2013). *Hackers and hacking: A reference handbook.* Santa Barbara, CA: ABC-CLIO.

Jolliffe, D., & Farrington, D. P. (2007). *A rapid evidence assessment of the impact of mentoring on re-offending.* London, UK: Home Office.

Keating, L., Tomishima, M., Foster, S., & Alessandri, M. (2002). The effects of a mentoring program on at-risk youth. *Adolescence, 37,* 717–734.

Lipsey, M. W., & Wilson, D. B. (1998). Effective intervention for serious juvenile offenders: A synthesis of research. In R. Loeber & D. Farrington (Eds.), *Serious and violent juvenile offenders: Risk factors and successful interventions* (pp. 313–341). Thousand Oaks, CA: Sage. https://doi.org/10.4135/9781452243740.n13.

Magnusson, D., & Stattin, H. (2006). The person in the environment: Towards a general model for scientific inquiry. In W. Damon & R. M. Lerner (Eds.), *Handbook of child psychology: Vol. 1. Theoretical models of human development* (6th ed., pp. 400–464). New York, NY: Wiley.

Matz, A. (2014). Commentary: Do youth mentoring programmes work? A review of the empirical literature. *Journal of Juvenile Justice, 3,* 88–106.

McDowell, D. J., Kim, M., O'Neil, R., & Parke, R. D. (2002). Children's emotional regulation and social competence in middle childhood: The role of maternal and paternal interactive style. *Marriage and Family Review, 34,* 345–364. https://doi.org/10.1300/J002v34n03_07.

Meyer, G. R. (1989). *The social organization of the computer underground.* Master's thesis. Retrieved from the National Institute of Standards and Technology Computer Security Resource Center (ADA390834).

Moodie, M. J., & Fisher, J. (2009). Are youth mentoring programs good value-for-money? An evaluation of the Big Brothers Big Sisters Melbourne Program. *BMC Public Health, 9*, 1–9. https://doi.org/10.1186/1471-2458-9-41.

Pawson, R. (2004). *Mentoring relationships: An explanatory review* (Working Paper 21). London, UK: ESRC UK Centre for Evidence Based Policy and Practice.

Radziszewska, B., & Rogoff, B. (1991). Children's guided participation in planning imaginary errands with skilled adult or peer partners. *Developmental Psychology, 27*, 381–389. https://doi.org/10.1037/0012-1649.27.3.381.

Rhodes, J. E. (2002). *Stand by me: The risks and rewards of mentoring today's youth*. Cambridge, MA: Harvard University Press.

Rhodes, J. E. (2005). A model of youth mentoring. In D. L. DuBois & M. J. Karcher (Eds.), *Handbook of youth mentoring* (pp. 30–43). Thousand Oaks, CA: Sage. https://doi.org/10.4135/9781412976664.n3.

Rhodes, J. (2008). Improving youth mentoring interventions through research-based practice. *American Journal of Community Psychology, 41*, 35–42. https://doi.org/10.1007/s10464-007-9153-9.

Royse, D. (1998). Mentoring high-risk minority youth: Evaluation of the Brothers project. *Adolescence, 33*, 145–158.

Scales, P. C., Benson, P. L., & Mannes, M. (2006). The contribution to adolescent well-being made by nonfamily adults: An examination of developmental assets as contexts and processes. *Journal of Community Psychology, 34*, 401–413. https://doi.org/10.1002/jcop.20106.

Schell, B. H., & Dodge, J. L. (2002). *The hacking of America: Who's doing it, why, and how*. Westport, CT: Quorum.

Skinner, W. F., & Fream, A. M. (1997). A social learning theory analysis of computer crime among college students. *Journal of Research in Crime and Delinquency, 34*, 495–518. https://doi.org/10.1177/0022427897034004005.

Smith, R. E., & Smoll, F. L. (2002). Youth sports as a behaviour setting for psychological interventions. In J. L. Van Raalte & B. W. Brewer (Eds.) *Exploring sport and exercise psychology* (pp 341–371). Washington, DC: American Psychological Association. https://doi.org/10.1037/10465-017.

Steinmetz, K. F. (2015). Craft(y)ness: An ethnographic study of hacking. *British Journal of Criminology, 55*, 125–145. https://doi.org/10.1093/bjc/azu061.

Tierney, J. P., Grossman, J. B., & Resch, N. L. (1995). *Making a difference: An impact study of Big Brothers Big Sisters*. Philadelphia, PA: Public/Private Ventures.

Tolan, P. H. (2002). Crime prevention: Focus on youth. In J. Q. Wilson & J. Petersilia (Eds.), *Crime* (pp. 109–128). Oakland, CA: Institute for Contemporary Studies Press.

Tolan, P. H., & Gorman-Smith, D. (2003). What violence prevention can tell us about developmental psychopathology. *Development and Psychopathology, 14*, 713–729. https://doi.org/10.1017/S0954579402004042.

Tolan, P. H., Henry, D., Schoeny, M., Bass, A. Lovegrove, P., & Nichols, E. (2013). Mentoring interventions to affect juvenile delinquency and associated problems: A systematic review. *Campbell Systematic Reviews, 10.* https://doi. org/10.4073/csr.2013.10.

Vygotsky, L. S. (1978). *Mind in society: The development of higher psychological processes.* Cambridge, MA: Harvard University Press.

Ware, V. (2013). *Mentoring programs for Indigenous youth at-risk* (Resource Sheet No. 22). Canberra, Australia: Australian Institute of Health and Welfare.

Weulen Kranenbarg, M., Holt, T. J., & Van Gelder, J.-L. (2019). Offending and victimization in the digital age: Comparing correlates of cybercrime and traditional offending-only, victimization-only and the victimization-offending overlap. *Deviant Behavior, 40*(1), 40–55. https://doi.org/10.1080/016396 25.2017.1411030.

CHAPTER 6

Targeted Warnings and Police Cautions

Abstract This chapter examines the use of targeted warnings and cautions by police (i.e. cease-and-desist messaging) that aim to deter potential offenders from future offending. These interventions rely on rational choice and labelling theories of crime. This chapter examines the results of studies that evaluate such interventions for offline crimes. Overall, we find that most of the evidence indicates qualified support for these interventions. Although cease-and-desist visits and targeted prevention messaging have been used in the context of cybercrime, there is little known about how effective they are. In exploring the applicability of these interventions to cybercrime, we highlight their limitations within digital contexts and provide recommendations for optimal design of this strategy for preventing cybercrime.

Keywords Labelling theory · Police cautions · Procedural justice · Rational choice theory · Reintegrative shaming theory · Targeted warnings

INTRODUCTION

Targeted warnings and cautions are used by police to warn potential offenders with the aim of deterring them from future offending. Though definitions of what constitutes such messaging can be broad, in this chapter we focus on stand-alone warnings, cautions, reprimands, and instructions to 'cease and desist', which may be carried out by law enforcement officers in person (e.g. on a home visit) or through letters. These may be 'formal' (i.e. recorded on a police computer system) or informal (i.e. no record being made). Excluded from the scope of this chapter are interventions delivered by a court, including cease-and-desist orders. Also excluded are similar interventions by other bodies, including private law firms, which often send 'cease and desist' letters for civil matters. Interventions that include additional actions, such as the referral to treatment or social services, have also generally been excluded.

This chapter first explores the various theories underpinning the efficacy of targeted warnings. Drawing from *rational choice theory*, these strategies are thought to prevent crime by increasing offenders' perceived threat of punishment for any future offence. *Labelling theory* provides an alternate mechanism for effects of such warnings on criminal activity. Although we find evidence that targeted warnings have been used in the context of cybercrime, there is little known about how effective they have been. This chapter, therefore, considers the empirical evidence for the utility of such interventions in relation to offline crimes. Overall, we find that most of the literature indicates qualified support for the intervention as applied to crime more broadly. Following this, we consider the utility of this intervention in preventing cybercrime. While this intervention has potential to be applied to the online context, we identify some possible limitations. Finally, we provide recommendations for optimal design of this strategy for preventing cybercrime.

THEORETICAL UNDERPINNINGS OF THE INTERVENTION

The intention of targeted warnings is to deter recipients from commencing, or continuing, offending, by imparting to the recipient that there is a cost to their activities, and a consequence if they continue down a criminal pathway. Two key theoretical perspectives underpin this type of intervention: deterrence and labelling. While these perspectives conflict, both offer rationales for crime prevention through diversion and warning.

The *deterrence* perspective, which originates from principles proposed by Beccaria (1764/2009), relies on rational choice models of crime, whereby individuals are seen as logical decision-makers who weigh up the potential costs and benefits of their actions. Punishment thus deters people from committing crime by elevating the costs of offending. Accordingly, issuing a warning to an individual who is beginning to show inclinations towards crime could potentially act as a deterrent by making punishment appear more *certain*—a key element of the deterrence model (Pratt et al. 2008).

On the other hand, *labelling theory* sees punishment as stigmatising, which can lead to further criminal activity (Becker 1963; Lemert 1967; Sherman et al. 1992b; Tittle 1995). Indeed, research has indicated that restrictive and deterrence-based sanctions can increase the likelihood of reoffending (Bernburg et al. 2006; Gatti et al. 2009; Koehler et al. 2013; Lipsey 2009; Petrosino et al. 2010; Smith et al. 2002). Labelling someone as an offender creates a self-fulfilling prophecy, in which individuals adopt criminal identities. Not only may others perceive that person as being a lawbreaker, placing them under greater scrutiny so that even minor transgressions are detected, but also that label may be internalised, and the individual may behave as they believe others see them. Therefore, by diverting a potential offender away from the criminal justice system, it is theorised that they are able to avoid the stigmatising effects of a court appearance.

Reintegrative shaming theory (Braithwaite 1989) provides some guidance as to which sanctions are likely to be more, or less, stigmatising. According to this perspective, sanctions that focus on the wrongfulness of (and harm caused by) the act, rather than the characteristics of the offender, are more likely to reduce crime. A related theory developed in the context of police behaviour is *procedural justice*, whereby people's compliance with the law is conditioned by their perceptions of fairness and legitimacy (Tyler 1990). These factors are critical in understanding the potential effectiveness of targeted warning interventions. Drawing from these theories, it is hypothesised that targeted warnings can prevent crime if the recipient perceives: (a) the warning as being fair; (b) the police officer who delivers the intervention as acting rightfully; and (c) the intervention is focused on the act rather than the actor.

Current Applications

Targeted warnings and cautions are examples of secondary crime prevention approaches, which intervene at the early stages of offending in order to avoid someone committing a crime or one that is more serious (Brantingham and Faust 1976). As such, they have traditionally been deployed in the context of less serious crimes, such as recreational drug use, or aimed at juveniles before the offending escalates to more serious criminal behaviour.

Substantial headway has been made in the UK with respect to the deployment of targeted approaches to warn those considered at risk of committing serious and organised crime, including cybercrime (Home Office 2018). This disruption activity has been delivered at scale on at least two occasions in the UK, targeting those believed to be in the early stages of committing cybercrime offences. In 2014, there was a UK-wide police investigation into *Blackshades*, a remote access tool designed to take over, control, and steal information from personal computers. The investigation resulted in 17 people being arrested and 80 receiving a visit from a police officer. Approximately 500 others received a warning letter advising that it was believed they had purchased the software and that using it could be illegal (BBC News 2015).

The following year, the database for the *LizardStresser* booter service, which provided denial of service attacks for a fee, was compromised and leaked. This database contained customer details for those who had purchased denial of service attacks from, or registered with, the service. Six individuals who had purchased denial of service attacks were subsequently arrested. Approximately 50 others who had registered with the site, but were not believed to have carried out an attack, received a home visit from the police (National Crime Agency 2015). Those receiving visits were told that denial of service attacks are 'illegal, can prevent individuals from accessing vital online services, and can cause significant financial and reputational damage to businesses' (National Crime Agency 2015, p. 1). They were also informed that 'committing cybercrime can result in severe restrictions on their freedom, access to the Internet, digital devices and future career prospects' (National Crime Agency 2015, p. 1).

There have also been coordinated international law enforcement actions involving users of a number of booter services. In 2016, Europol's European Cybercrime Centre coordinated law enforcement authorities from Australia, Belgium, France, Hungary, Lithuania, the Netherlands, Norway, Portugal, Romania, Spain, Sweden, the UK, and the USA. Overall, 34 individuals were arrested, and 101 suspects were interviewed and cautioned (Europol 2016).

Despite differences in their method of delivery, the objectives of these interventions were quite similar. The interventions were aimed at people already involved in cybercrime or at least on the periphery.

For example, it would not have been a crime to create an account with the *LizardStresser* service or even to use it to test one's own systems. However, using it against another target without permission would be considered a criminal offence in many jurisdictions. Therefore, registering with the website may be considered a warning sign of awareness of such criminal services and contemplation of their use. Consequently, in these cases, the targeted warnings aimed to reduce the frequency or severity of offending, if not to stop it altogether.

EVIDENCE BASE FOR THE INTERVENTION

At the time of writing, we were unable to locate any empirical evidence pointing to the effectiveness of targeted caution interventions in reducing cybercrime. There is, however, a wealth of evidence for the use of targeted cautions in the offline context. Most of the evidence indicated qualified support for the use of cautions or warnings for identified offenders and those at risk of offending. It should be noted that in many cases, cautions are considered a control condition for the purposes of evaluating the effects of a different type of intervention (e.g. a court program). Given this, it would be an insurmountable task to locate every single study utilising cautions as at least one of the experimental conditions. Nevertheless, we have included these where possible.

A meta-analysis of 14 studies revealed that caution or warning interventions were more effective than traditional criminal justice processing at reducing recidivism among adolescent offenders (Wilson and Hoge 2013). In fact, the effect found for simple cautions was equivalent in size to that found for more comprehensive intervention programs (e.g. referral to support services and treatment). However, most of the caution evaluations employed a weak methodological design.

An early study, and also one of the most rigorous, was conducted by McBride and Peck (1970) who evaluated warning letters delivered to 18,000 negligent drivers. They randomly allocated drivers into a number of experimental groups, as well as a control group who received no letter. The experimental groups either received a standard letter, which was already in use, or one manipulated to change the intimacy of style or degree of threat. Participants who received any warning letter were less likely to be detected committing further violations, though the best effects were found for those that received low-threat or standard letters.

Chapman et al. (1994) also used random allocation into control and experimental conditions to evaluate the effects of warning letters on the illegal sale of tobacco products to underage children by retail outlets. Undercover buying operations were conducted three months apart, with half of the shops that sold to minors on the first occasion receiving a warning letter. The letter stated that they had been recorded as having sold cigarettes to children and that at an unspecified date in the future, children would again be sent unannounced into their shop to attempt to purchase cigarettes. The letter warned that if they were identified selling tobacco to those underage on a second occasion, they could be prosecuted. Shops which sold on the first occasion and received warning letters reduced selling by 69%, although the control group also had a 40% reduction.

Mazerolle et al. (1998) differed from the other studies considered here, as they used place as the unit of analysis, rather than individuals. Specifically, they researched the effectiveness of civil remedies for properties in Oakland, California, that were reported as having drug crime and disorder problems. The experimental condition included warning letters, along with inspections, evictions, and property clean-ups, while those randomly allocated to the control condition faced traditional police tactics, including surveillance, arrests, and field interrogations. The research team observed each site twice before the intervention, and twice after, to measure changes in street behaviour. They found that the locations assigned to the treatment condition had less observed drug dealing and fewer signs of disorder after the intervention, compared to the control group.

In the Milwaukee Domestic Violence Experiment (Sherman et al. 1992a), police dispatchers randomly allocated eligible cases of domestic violence into one of three groups: (1) full arrest, in which the suspect was eligible for release on $250 bail; (2) short arrest, in which suspects were released as soon as possible and preferably within two hours; and (3) warning, in which the suspect was not arrested, but was read a standard warning indicating they would be arrested if the police had to return that evening. Sherman et al. (1992a) found that there was an initial deterrent effect, in which both short and full arrest groups had fewer instances of repeated violence, compared to the warning group. However, in the long term, arrest had an escalating effect, with arrest increasing the risk of violence compared to warnings. Therefore, warnings seemed to be more effective than arrests.

More recently, Sherman and Harris (2015) published a follow-up study on the Milwaukee Domestic Violence Experiment. Rather than measuring reoffending, this particular analysis compared the death rates of the victims of domestic assault, whose partners had been randomly allocated to either receive a warning or be arrested. They found that 23 years later, if the abuser had been arrested, the victim was 64% more likely to have died than those whose partners had been warned. However, in total, only three homicides were recorded (two in the arrest group, one in the warning group), with other causes of death including alcohol and drugs, cancer, and heart disease. Due to the low incidence of the relevant outcome (intimate partner homicide), this later study only provides weak evidence in favour of targeted warnings.

A number of other less rigorous studies also provide evidence in favour of targeted warning interventions (Allard et al. 2010; Baker and Goh 2004; Bazemore et al. 2004; Dennison et al. 2006; Kraus 1981; Vignaendra and Fitzgerald 2006; Wang and Weatherburn 2019). The main limitation of these evaluations is there is no random allocation. Therefore, there may be key differences between the groups that received the intervention and those that did not.

In addition to the favourable research cited above, a number of studies have found no significant difference in later offending for those who received a warning, rather than another type of intervention (Mott 1983; Shanahan et al. 2017; Shirley 2017; Wilcox et al. 2004). These studies, however, had a number of methodological limitations, so they should not be weighted as heavily as those further above. We also identified research that was not supportive of targeted warnings (Galeazzi et al. 2009; Storey and Hart 2011; Willner et al. 2000). These studies also had severe shortcomings, with both Galeazzi et al. (2009) and Storey and Hart (2011), relying exclusively on subjective perceptions of caution strategies.

Overall, the evidence considered here indicates that cautions and warnings can have a beneficial effect on reducing offending, at least for some offence types and populations. However, moderating variables might enhance the effectiveness of targeted warning interventions. McBride and Peck (1970) claim that the way cautions are delivered can play an important role. For example, the language used and information provided may have an impact on outcomes. Paternoster et al. (1997) analysed data from the Milwaukee Domestic Violence Experiment for evidence of procedural justice and perceptions of fairness and legitimacy, which, as previously mentioned, can have an effect on compliance with the law (Tyler 1990). Here, the authors examined interview data of arrested offenders, coding for whether those arrested believed the officers had taken the time to listen to their side of the story, if they had expected to be arrested, and if the officers had listened to their story as well as the victim's story. They found that perceived procedural justice was important to outcomes, as individuals who were arrested and perceived that they had been treated unfairly had higher recidivism rates than those who were warned. Subsequent assault rates for those who were arrested but believed they had been treated fairly were similar as those who had been warned.

Similarly, targeted cautions may have potential unintended effects that reduce their effectiveness. Of particular note, there is the potential for *net-widening* with the use of cautions, as noted by at least one study (see Baker and Goh 2004). Net-widening refers to more individuals being included within interventions than originally intended. The effect is to move the goalposts so that police take action at a lower threshold (Decker 1985). Therefore, rather than diverting people from the criminal justice system, other individuals are drawn in for relatively minor transgressions, meaning they could face more stigmatisation than they would have otherwise and be more likely to face court later. Therefore, net-widening that might occur through encouraging the use of cautions may actually increase the likelihood of future offending.

Compounding this problem, cautions may, in some cases, result in defiance—the antithesis to the re-integrative shaming approach (Sherman 1993). If the recipient of a warning perceives it as being unfair or disrespectful, they may defy the warning given and even become a more persistent offender, increasing in frequency and/or seriousness. Where cautions are issued for behaviours that are considered legitimate by the recipient (e.g. behaviour that is not illegal), defiance may follow. Furthermore, a caution might be seen as a 'badge of honour', which glamorises criminal status (Hodgkinson and Tilley 2007). In such cases, the effect of the intervention would not be to deter the recipient, but rather to enhance their standing with peers. It is, therefore, important to carefully consider the scope and target of caution strategies.

FUTURE APPLICATIONS AND ADAPTATIONS TO DIGITAL CONTEXTS

Targeted warnings and cautions have qualified support in the offline context. However, these findings may not be generalisable to cybercrime offenders for a number of reasons. Though there has been no published evaluation of this type of approach by law enforcement when applied to cybercrime offenders, we consider below factors that are likely to be applicable in this context.

The observation that offenders who engage in different types of crime may be more, or less, amenable to deterrence was an issue of interest to Chambliss (1967). He reviewed the evidence on drug addiction, parking law violations, white-collar crime, and shoplifting, hypothesising that deterrability depends on the type of act and degrees of commitment to crime. The most likely to be deterred include those who have a low commitment to crime but do it for instrumental reasons, such as white-collar criminals, while the least likely to be deterred are people with a high commitment to 'expressive' crimes, such as drug and sex offences. Research suggests that many types of cybercrime are committed for instrumental purposes, such as money or peer recognition (Hutchings 2016). If this is the case, then well-targeted cautions that increase offenders' perceptions of the likelihood of detection could be a promising strategy.

The characteristics of the offender may also affect the outcomes. Green (1985) evaluated warning letters sent from a cable company (i.e. not by police) to people identified as stealing premium cable television. By inspecting the terminals connected to subscribers' homes, the researchers were able to detect basic subscribers who had installed devices to descramble the signals of premium services. Following the intervention, the evaluation found that the most common reaction to the warning letter was to remove the descrambler, while one-third of recipients took no action. Follow-up inspections indicated that the least deterred were men, the youngest (those aged 18–25), and those who were most affluent. This finding is important to consider in respect to cybercrime, as young men make up the most common demographic (Hutchings and Chua 2017).

The role of peer recognition in cybercrime makes the use of cautions a potentially problematic approach. Being the recipient of a caution, particularly something that can be displayed, such as a letter, may be perceived as a 'badge of honour' (Hodgkinson and Tilley 2007). In addition, online communities may provide a strong source of legitimacy to justify individuals' cybercrime activities, such that recipients of a caution they view as illegitimate may respond with defiance. As Paternoster et al. (1997) found, the success of any intervention could depend on the details of delivery and the recipients' perceptions of legitimacy and procedural justice.

Other potential unintended effects of this type of intervention include enticement, displacement, creative adaptation, and chilling effects. When it comes to enticement, the 'forbidden fruit effect' (see, e.g., Grabosky 1996) may induce those being warned to try out the illicit behaviour. This can occur through outright rebellion on behalf of the recipient, inciting their curiosity or highlighting the potential of an action to which they were previously oblivious. Crime displacement occurs when crime moves to other locations, times, targets, methods, perpetrators, or offences, as the result of crime prevention initiatives (Smith et al. 2003). Some crime prevention strategies—including targeted warnings and cautions—may cause offenders to refine their avoidance behaviour. This is particularly relevant to cybercrime, as different and changing technologies proffer tools enabling creative adaptation (Grabosky 1996), where innovative offenders can change their behaviour so they are harder to catch in the future. Lastly, interventions may also harm the general law-abiding population (Grabosky 1996). For example, electronic surveillance can have a 'chilling effect' on Internet use more generally (Schneier 2015). This includes individuals avoiding searching for information on potentially sensitive topics, such as health, sexuality, or religion.

On the other hand, offenders interviewed by Hutchings (2016) also indicated that it was the likelihood of detection, not the severity of punishment, that mattered to them. Therefore, warnings and cautions may be useful in highlighting that low-level offenders are not necessarily anonymous online, increasing the perceived likelihood of detection.

The research reviewed in this chapter provides some insights into what best practice may look like for warnings and cautions in the cybercrime context. First, the intervention should highlight the costs of offending (e.g. to future career prospects) but avoid threatening language. Second, it is best to focus on the wrongfulness of the act, rather than the actor (e.g. avoid stigmatisation). Third, those delivering the intervention should take time to listen to the recipient, hearing their side of the story, and treat them fairly and respectfully.

REFERENCES

Allard, T., Stewart, A., Chrzanowski, A., Ogilvie, J., Birks, D., & Little, S. (2010). *Police diversion of young offenders and Indigenous over-representation* (Trends and Issues in Crime and Criminal Justice, No. 390). Canberra, Australia: Australian Institute of Criminology.

Baker, J., & Goh, D. (2004). *Cannabis Cautioning Scheme three years on: An implementation & outcome evaluation*. Sydney, Australia: New South Wales Bureau of Crime Statistics and Research.

Bazemore, G., Stinchcomb, J. B., & Leip, L. A. (2004). Scared smart or bored straight? Testing deterrence logic in an evaluation of police-led truancy intervention. *Justice Quarterly, 21*(2), 269–299. https://doi.org/10.1080/07418820400095811.

BBC News. (2015). *Police target UK's young cybercriminals*. Available at http://www.bbc.co.uk/news/technology-35028690. Accessed 1 Oct 2018.

Beccaria, C. (2009). *On crimes and punishments* (G. R. Newman & P. Marongiu, Trans.). New Brunswick, NJ: Transaction Publishers. (Original work published 1764.)

Becker, H. S. (1963). *Outsiders*. New York, NY: The Free Press.

Bernburg, J. G., Krohn, M. D., & Rivera, C. J. (2006). Official labeling, criminal embeddedness, and subsequent delinquency: A longitudinal test of labeling theory. *Journal of Research in Crime and Delinquency, 43*, 67–88. https://doi.org/10.1177/0022427805280068.

Braithwaite, J. (1989). *Crime, shame and reintegration*. Cambridge, UK: Cambridge University Press. https://doi.org/10.1017/cbo9780511804618.

Brantingham, P. J., & Faust, F. L. (1976). A conceptual model of crime prevention. *Crime and Delinquency, 22*(3), 284–296. https://doi.org/10.1177/001112877602200302.

Chambliss, W. J. (1967). Types of deviance and the effectiveness of legal sanctions. *Wisconsin Law Review, 1967*(3), 703–719.

Chapman, S., King, M., Andrews, B., McKay, E., Markham, P., & Woodward, S. (1994). Effects of publicity and a warning letter on illegal cigarette sales to minors. *Australian and New Zealand Journal of Public Health, 18*(1), 39–42. https://doi.org/10.1111/j.1753-6405.1994.tb00192.x.

Decker, S. H. (1985). A systematic analysis of diversion: Net widening and beyond. *Journal of Criminal Justice, 13*(3), 207–216. https://doi.org/10.1016/0047-2352(85)90099-6.

Dennison, S., Stewart, A., & Hurren, E. (2006). *Police cautioning in Queensland: The impact on juvenile offending pathways* (Trends and Issues in Crime and Criminal Justice, No. 306). Canberra, Australia: Australian Institute of Criminology.

Europol. (2016). *Joint international operation targets young users of DDoS cyber-attack tools.* Available at https://www.europol.europa.eu/newsroom/news/joint-international-operation-targets-young-users-of-ddos-cyber-attack-tools. Accessed 25 May 2019.

Galeazzi, G. M., Bučar-Ručman, A., DeFazio, L., & Groenen, A. (2009). Experiences of stalking victims and requests for help in three European countries: A survey. *European Journal on Criminal Policy and Research, 15*(3), 243–260. https://doi.org/10.1007/s10610-009-9102-2.

Gatti, U., Tremblay, R. E., & Vitaro, F. (2009). Iatrogenic effect of juvenile justice. *Journal of Child Psychology and Psychiatry, 50,* 991–998. https://doi.org/10.1111/j.1469-7610.2008.02057.x.

Grabosky, P. N. (1996). Unintended consequences of crime prevention. *Crime Prevention Studies, 5,* 25–56.

Green, G. S. (1985). General deterrence and television cable crime: A field experiment in social control. *Criminology, 23*(4), 629–645. https://doi.org/10.1111/j.1745-9125.1985.tb00367.x.

Hodgkinson, S., & Tilley, N. (2007). Policing anti-social behaviour: Constraints, dilemmas and opportunities. *The Howard Journal of Criminal Justice, 46*(4), 385–400. https://doi.org/10.1111/j.1468-2311.2007.00484.x.

Home Office. (2018). *Serious and organised crime strategy.* London, UK: The Stationary Office.

Hutchings, A. (2016). Cybercrime trajectories: An integrated theory of initiation, maintenance, and desistance. In T. J. Holt (Ed.), *Crime online: Correlates, causes, and context* (pp. 117–140). Durham, UK: Caroline Academic Press.

Hutchings, A., & Chua, Y. T. (2017). Gendering cybercrime. In T. J. Holt (Ed.), *Cybercrime through an interdisciplinary lens* (pp. 167–188). Abingdon, Oxon, UK: Routledge.

Koehler, J. A., Lösel, F., Akoensi, T. D., & Humphreys, D. K. (2013). A systematic review and meta-analysis on the effects of young offender treatment programs in Europe. *Journal of Experimental Criminology, 9,* 19–43. https://doi.org/10.1007/s11292-012-9159-7.

Kraus, J. (1981). Police caution of juvenile offenders: A research note. *Australian and New Zealand Journal of Criminology, 14*(2), 91–94. https://doi.org/10.1177/000486588101400204.

Lemert, E. M. (1967). *Human deviance, social problems, and social control.* Englewood Cliffs, NJ: Prentice Hall.

Lipsey, M. W. (2009). The primary factors that characterize effective interventions with juvenile offenders: A meta-analytic overview. *Victims and Offenders, 4,* 124–147. https://doi.org/10.1080/15564880802612573.

Mazerolle, L. G., Roehl, J., & Kadleck, C. (1998). Controlling social disorder using civil remedies: Results from a randomized field experiment in Oakland, California. *Crime Prevention Studies, 9,* 141–159.

McBride, R. S., & Peck, R. C. (1970). Modifying negligent driving behavior through warning letters. *Accident Analysis and Prevention, 2*(3), 147–174. https://doi.org/10.1016/0001-4575(70)90048-5.

Mott, J. (1983). Police decisions for dealing with juvenile offenders. *The British Journal of Criminology, 23*(3), 249–262. https://doi.org/10.1093/oxfordjournals.bjc.a047378.

National Crime Agency. (2015). *Operation Vivarium targets users of Lizard Squad's website attack tool.* Available at http://www.nationalcrimeagency.gov.uk/news/691-operation-vivarium-targets-users-of-lizard-squad-s-website-attack-tool. Accessed 1 Oct 2018.

Paternoster, R., Brame, R., Bachman, R., & Sherman, L. W. (1997). Do fair procedures matter? The effect of procedural justice on spouse assault. *Law and Society Review, 31*(1), 163–204. https://doi.org/10.2307/3054098.

Petrosino, A., Turpin-Petrosino, C., & Guckenburg, S. (2010). Formal system processing of juveniles: Effects on delinquency. *Campbell Systematic Reviews, 1.* https://doi.org/10.4073/csr.2010.1.

Pratt, T. C., Cullen, F. T., Blevins, K. R., Daigle, L. E., & Madensen, T. D. (2008). The empirical status of deterrence theory: A meta-analysis. In F. T. Cullen, J. P. Wright, & K. R. Blevins (Eds.), *Taking stock: The status of criminological theory* (pp. 367–396). New Brunswick, NJ: Transaction Publishers. https://doi.org/10.4324/9781315130620-14.

Schneier, B. (2015). *Data and Goliath: The hidden battles to collect your data and control your world.* New York, NY: W. W. Norton.

Shanahan, M., Hughes, C. E., McSweeney, T., & Griffin, B. A. (2017). Alternate policing strategies: Cost-effectiveness of cautioning for cannabis offences. *International Journal of Drug Policy, 41,* 140–147. https://doi.org/10.1016/j.drugpo.2016.12.012.

Shirley, K. (2017). *The cautious approach: Police cautions and the impact on youth reoffending* (Brief No. 9). Melbourne, Australia: Crime Statistics Agency.

Sherman, L. W. (1993). Defiance, deterrence, and irrelevance: A theory of the criminal sanction. *Journal of Research in Crime and Delinquency, 30*(4), 445–473. https://doi.org/10.1177/0022427893030004006.

Sherman, L. W., & Harris, H. M. (2015). Increased death rates of domestic violence victims from arresting vs. warning suspects in the Milwaukee Domestic Violence Experiment (MilDVE). *Journal of Experimental Criminology, 11*(1), 1–20. https://doi.org/10.1007/s11292-014-9203-x.

Sherman, L. W., Schmidt, J. D., Rogan, D. P., Smith, D. A., Gartin, P. R., Cohn, E. G., et al. (1992a). The variable effects of arrest on criminal careers: The Milwaukee domestic violence experiment. *The Journal of Criminal Law and Criminology, 83,* 137–169. https://doi.org/10.2307/1143827.

Sherman, L. W., Smith, D. A., Schmidt, J. D., & Rogan, D. P. (1992b). Crime, punishment, and stake in conformity: Legal and informal control of domestic violence. *American Sociological Review,* *57*(5), 680–690. https://doi.org/10.2307/2095921.

Smith, R. E., & Smoll, F. L. (2002). Youth sports as a behaviour setting for psychological interventions. In J. L. Van Raalte & B. W. Brewer (Eds.) *Exploring sport and exercise psychology* (pp 341–371). Washington, DC: American Psychological Association. https://doi.org/10.1037/10465-017.

Smith, R. G., Wolanin, N., & Worthington, G. (2003). *e-Crime solutions and crime displacement* (Trends and Issues in Crime and Criminal Justice, No. 243). Canberra, Australia: Australian Institute of Criminology.

Storey, J. E., & Hart, S. D. (2011). How do police respond to stalking? An examination of the risk management strategies and tactics used in a specialized anti-stalking law enforcement unit. *Journal of Police and Criminal Psychology, 26*(2), 128–142. https://doi.org/10.1007/s11896-010-9081-8.

Tittle, C. R. (1995). *Control balance: Toward a general theory of deviance.* Boulder, CO: Westview Press.

Tyler, T. R. (1990). *Why people obey the law.* New Haven, CT: Yale University Press.

Vignaendra, S., & Fitzgerald, J. (2006). Reoffending among young people cautioned by police or who participated in a youth justice conference. *Crime and Justice Bulletin, 103,* 1–15.

Wang, J. J., & Weatherburn, D. (2019). Are police cautions a soft option? Reoffending among juveniles cautioned or referred to court. *Australian and New Zealand Journal of Criminology, 52*(3), 334–347. https://doi.org/10.1177/0004865818794235.

Wilcox, A., Young, R., & Hoyle, C. (2004). *Two-year resanctioning study: A comparison of restorative & traditional caution.* London, UK: Home Office.

Wilson, H. A., & Hoge, R. D. (2013). The effect of youth diversion programs on recidivism: A meta-analytic review. *Criminal Justice and Behavior, 40,* 497–518. https://doi.org/10.1177/0093854812451089.

Willner, P., Hart, K., Binmore, J., Cavendish, M., & Dunphy, E. (2000). Alcohol sales to underage adolescents: An unobtrusive observational field study and evaluation of a police intervention. *Addiction, 95*(9), 1373–1388. https://doi.org/10.1046/j.1360-0443.2000.95913738.x.

PART III

Tertiary Forms of Prevention

CHAPTER 7

Positive Diversions

Abstract This chapter examines the programs and strategies associated with positive diversions. Positive diversions redirect individuals towards prosocial behaviours and peer influences and focus on rehabilitation rather than punitive actions. This chapter reviews the evidence for such interventions in reducing offline crime, concluding that the findings are mixed, with some diversions showing positive effects and others showing negative effects. We then explore the applicability of diversions to cybercrime prevention, finding that though there is no research evidence for the effectiveness of such, there is some anecdotal evidence that redirecting cybercriminals into cybersecurity programs or training could be beneficial. We conclude by delineating what an ideal diversion program could look like for cybercriminals, drawing out the factors that would likely lead to its success in the digital realm.

Keywords Academic programs · Cultural arts programs · Peer contagion · Positive diversions · Sports programs · Wilderness camps

INTRODUCTION

This chapter examines the programs and strategies associated with positive diversions. Diversions are strategies that redirect a person away from traditional criminal justice procedures and sanctions. More specifically,

© The Author(s) 2019   93
R. Brewer et al., *Cybercrime Prevention*,
Crime Prevention and Security Management,
https://doi.org/10.1007/978-3-030-31069-1_7

positive diversions can be understood as redirection towards interventions that enhance young people's well-being and social inclusion (Haines et al. 2012; Smith 2014). That is, positive diversions aim to foster positive attitudes, peers, and behaviours through a more rehabilitative approach to risk management. Positive diversions can take a variety of forms, including art, sports, and outdoors programs. We exclude from consideration strictly psychotherapeutic interventions (e.g. counselling), though these may form part of a positive diversion strategy. Instead, we focus on broader programming that is aimed at enhancing individuals' peer and social context.

This chapter reviews the evidence for such interventions in reducing offline crime, concluding that the findings are mixed, with some diversions showing positive effects and others showing negative effects. More specifically, we examine some of the most widely deployed diversion programs, drawing out the factors that lead to their success and some potential pitfalls. We then explore the applicability of positive diversions to cybercrime, finding that though there is no research evidence for the effectiveness of such, there is some anecdotal evidence that redirecting cyber-offenders into cybersecurity programs or training could be beneficial. We conclude by delineating what an ideal diversion program could look like for cyber-offenders, drawing out the factors that would likely lead to its success in the digital realm.

THEORETICAL UNDERPINNINGS OF THE INTERVENTION

Imposing traditional criminal justice sanctions on young people has, at best, little effect on reoffending; at worst, restrictive and deterrence-based sanctions can *increase* the likelihood of youth reoffending (Bernburg et al. 2006; Gatti et al. 2009; Koehler et al. 2013; Lipsey 2009; Petrosino et al. 2010; Smith et al. 2002). Diversions, therefore, attempt to avoid the criminogenic effect of these processes (e.g. via labelling and peer contagion) by disposing people into alternate pathways before they come into formal contact with the criminal justice system.

Positive diversions are situated in a social context, seeking to tackle the underlying causes of youth offending by providing mechanisms to promote prosocial and positive behaviour (Haines and Case 2015). At the very minimum, positive diversions attempt to bond offenders back to communities by connecting them with prosocial activities. Through this, it is hoped that offenders will develop alternative, prosocial identities that are diametrically opposed to criminal identities and can, therefore, act as motivators to avoid criminal behaviour. Thus, positive diversions lean heavily on social bond theories of crime, which claim that genuine attachment to families, peers, and social institutions are critical in preventing crime (Hirschi 1969; Uggen and Wakefield 2005).

Though there is little doubt that antisocial attitudes and beliefs are strongly related to youth reoffending (Grieger and Hosser 2014; McGrath and Thompson 2012; Simourd and Andrews 1994), simply placing youths into social courses is in most cases likely insufficient to modify antisocial behaviour. Thus, many diversion programs incorporate more active strategies to foster prosocial attitudes and behaviours by drawing on social-cognitive principles of behaviour change (Bandura 1971; Turner and Oakes 1986). For example, programs can model prosocial attitudes and behaviours; provide incentives for, and reward, positive behaviours; appeal to role models that are relevant to potential offenders' self-concepts (e.g. ex-offenders) to motivate change; and challenge antisocial attitudes and beliefs through cognitive-behavioural techniques.

CURRENT APPLICATIONS

Diversions, in general, have traditionally been used for young people and first-time offenders (Smith 2014), targeting individuals deemed to be at risk of offending before their behaviour escalates into serious criminal behaviour (i.e. it is a secondary prevention measure). For example, programs may target troubled youth who have shown antisocial behaviour or have had some contact with the police but not yet committed serious offences. The logic for this targeting is as follows: if contact with the criminal justice system is criminogenic, it is more efficacious to divert a person from first contact with the criminal justice system rather than later down the track when a person has already had extensive exposure to the criminal justice system. Thus, the aim of diversion is to reduce the number of first-time entrants to the criminal justice system (Smith 2014).

In practice, diversions may be a substitute for criminal sanctions or court proceedings or be an accompaniment to such processes. Note, however, that to minimise criminogenic effects, in line with the theory underpinning the intervention, diversion should avoid contact with the criminal justice system as much possible in order to minimise exposure to delinquent peers or labelling. Diversions, in general, may thus vary in criminogenic potential, from informal cautions (potentially least criminogenic with a low risk of peer contagion and stigmatising labelling) through to prison-like residential placements (potentially most criminogenic with a high risk of peer contagion and labelling).

Turning to positive diversions specifically, to date there is no evidence that systematic programming has been implemented to deal with cybercrime, though there is anecdotal evidence that some notorious cyber-offenders have been able to transition their skills from criminal pursuits to legitimate security jobs, such as Kevin Mitnick, Peiter 'Mudge' Zatko, and Kevin Poulsen (see, e.g., Mitnick and Simon 2011). In contrast, positive diversions (and diversions more generally) have been widely deployed in response to various low-severity crimes and general delinquency. Due to the potential criminogenic effects of contact with the criminal justice system, and the reduced emphasis of retribution in positive diversions, normally only less serious offences are considered suitable for diversion from formal legal sanctions. This is consistent with the risk principle of offender intervention: less intensive, minimal interventions should be used with low-risk individuals (Andrews et al. 1990a). However, some more intensive diversions (e.g. those that involve a residential placement) have been used for more serious offences, often in place of incarceration.

EVIDENCE BASE FOR INTERVENTION

It is difficult to make broad claims about the effectiveness of diversions in general. Two meta-analyses of diversion programs (comparing diversion programs to traditional criminal justice processes) have been undertaken with mixed findings. Schwalbe et al. (2012) conducted a meta-analysis of 28 studies of mostly Caucasian male first-time/minor offenders (mean offender age 14.2 years) and found that there was no effect on reoffending, except for a single positive effect if the diversion was family treatment. However, this study included 'minimal intervention' (incorporating cautions) as a control group (versus diversion) because it only considered more intensive diversions in the treatment group. Therefore, the findings can only suggest that intensive diversions are no more effective than formal justice processing *or* minimal intervention.

In contrast, a larger meta-analysis conducted by Wilson and Hoge (2013)—45 studies, mean age 14.7, also mostly male and Caucasian, mainly low-risk property offenders—found diversions reduced reoffending. Notably, the authors included cautions (i.e. a minimal intervention) as a diversion rather than as a control group. Moreover, diversions that were a condition of a traditional disposition were excluded. Thus, the analysis in this study is a better reflection of the effects of diversion proper. Results indicated that recidivism depended on a number of factors. Specifically, diversions were more effective for those who could be considered low risk (e.g. those diverted without receiving a formal criminal charge and low in criminogenic need). There are two things that could be suggested here: one, that *no* treatment is better than any program (diversion or otherwise) or two, that diversions are more effective for those with less chronic or less severe dysfunction.

It must be remembered, however, that both reviews included a range of diversion programs, including restorative justice, drug courts, and psychotherapeutic treatment programs (not included in the current definition of positive diversions). Effects are likely to vary depending on the type of program and services offered; thus, considering these programs separately is more meaningful than relying on an average effect of diversion (e.g. Lipsey 2009). Focusing specifically now on positive diversions, some of the most popular programs are reviewed below.

To begin with, one of the most well-known positive diversions, *wilderness camps*, involve structured group-based physical challenges in an outdoor environment (e.g. trekking, rock climbing). These are distinct from punitive boot camps that attempt to instil discipline in young people through military training regimes. Though boot camps are a diversion to some extent (i.e. they often replace custodial sentences), they focus on the suppression of negative behaviours and use punishment and humiliation to try to change behaviour. Therefore, they are not a *positive* diversion (and generally, they are not effective at reducing criminal behaviour) (Drake et al. 2009; Lipsey 2009; Meade and Steiner 2010; Wilson et al. 2005). In contrast, wilderness camps are rehabilitative and constructive in orientation. The rationale of such programs is that mastering challenges facilitates personal growth through the development of self-efficacy, self-control, and interpersonal skills. A meta-analysis of 22 studies (mostly male Caucasians between the ages of 13 and 15, who were on probation and/or adjudicated delinquents) indicated that wilderness programs have a modest effect on recidivism for antisocial or delinquent youth (Wilson and Lipsey 2000). Programs were more effective when they were explicitly complemented by therapeutic components. These findings suggest that the positive skills and capacities developed through structured challenge activities can form the basis for behaviour change for more moderate-risk individuals—alongside therapeutic treatment.

Sports and recreation programs are also widely deployed. They aim to keep youths busy, build positive character/values, and foster lasting social bonds. However, robust evaluations for sports and recreation programs are lacking, so it is unclear whether such programs are effective at preventing delinquency. A recent meta-analysis found no effect of sports participation *in general* (i.e. programs may include non-delinquents) on crime (Spruit et al. 2016). Indeed, some commentators argue that sports programs are unlikely to have direct effects on crime and that such programs must be integrated with health, welfare, and other support services (Coalter 2013; Morris et al. 2003). In line with this, many sports programs have moved away from sports as simply a use of leisure time, to sports as a *process* that can facilitate change through positive social climate, and supportive, reinforcing relationships (Coalter 2013). Though this is a step in the right direction, without demonstrated effects on crime it is possible that some sports programs are ineffective, or at worst, counterproductive. Sports, unlike wilderness camps, are inherently competitive, which may work against the desired outcome of positive peer interaction. Moreover, Spruit et al. (2016) suggest that some sports have an alcohol consumption culture, which could interfere with positive program effects. Though it is important to consider how recreation activities may provide enjoyment, confidence, and purpose for young people— worthwhile goals in isolation perhaps—in terms of reoffending, some of these programs may carry hidden risks.

Robust evaluations of *cultural arts programs* (e.g. visual art, drama, dance) are similarly scant but there is some evidence that they can be effective in some cases. Theoretically, arts-based programs can provide an outlet for expressing and addressing emotional and cognitive problems (including those that are related to individuals' offending), while learning skills and developing a sense of mastery and purpose. Generally, arts programs have a weak theoretical basis and have been poorly implemented/evaluated (Rapp-Paglicci et al. 2006). However, there are some exceptions. Reading for Life is a 16-week literature-based diversion program for non-violent juvenile offenders in the USA, designed to foster character development in at-risk adolescents through moral discussions about characters and narratives. It is facilitated by trained volunteer facilitators who also act as prosocial role models and mentors. A robust randomised control trial of 418 young offenders (average age 15–16 years) found that the program had a sizeable effect on rearrests, even at two years follow-up (Seroczynski et al. 2016). The program may have been effective because it targeted antisocial cognition—a strong predictor of youth recidivism (Grieger and Hosser 2014; McGrath and Thompson 2012; Simourd and Andrews 1994)—through cognitive-behavioural techniques, such as cognitive restricting.

Similarly, a drama-based program in the USA was designed to build young offenders' perspective-taking skills in order to facilitate empathy and moral development. In small groups, youth were asked to develop, portray, and record brief skits relevant to their age group. The program was evaluated based on a sample of chronic delinquent boys (defined as those who had lengthy police and court records, and had committed crimes which would have constituted felonies were they adults). Aged 11–13 years, and mostly African American, these boys were randomised to the treatment group, a *placebo* group (drama but without the perspective-taking instruction/orientation of the treatment group), and a control group. Significant reductions in delinquency at 18-month follow-up were found only for the treatment group (Chandler 1973). However, the study was limited by the very small sample size (only about 10–15 in each group), and the applicability to the current context is questionable as the boys were serious offenders. Nevertheless, though the findings are tentative, they suggest that arts-based positive diversions may be effective when they actively target criminogenic risk factors (e.g. antisocial cognition). The arts framework itself provides a *vehicle* for the social-cognitive strategies to be communicated and practised. Though the art component itself might attract, retain, and motivate young people by appealing to their interests and capacities—an important consideration for any program (Andrews et al. 1990a)—it is unlikely to be the active ingredient in reducing recidivism.

Academic and vocational programs are hypothesised to provide skills and qualifications that can lead to the adoption of prosocial roles in society, while increasing the costs of reoffending (i.e. having 'more to lose'; Andrews et al. 1990b, p. 375). Moreover, such interventions may bolster protective factors, such as involvement with prosocial peers and activities. In line with the logic of these programs, research has found that poor education and unemployment are risk factors for delinquency (Grieger and Hosser 2014; Lipsey and Derzon 1998; Maguin and Loeber 1996; McGrath and Thompson 2012; Simourd and Andrews 1994). This is particularly the case for low-risk offenders (Gavazzi et al. 2008).

Academic and vocational interventions have been demonstrated to have relatively small effects on youth reoffending, with academic programs faring better than employment programs (Lipsey 2009). However, some scholars have argued that there is a *spurious relationship* between academic/vocational performance and delinquency: traits such as impulsiveness and low self-control might lead to *both* poor academic/vocational performance *and* delinquency and could be responsible for much of the relationship between them (Felson and Staff 2006; Maguin and Loeber 1996). This might explain the limited effects of educational and vocational programs. It is simply too much to ask troubled young people to adopt prosocial roles and identities when they lack the fundamental capacities to do so effectively. Clearly, providing meaningful opportunities for advancement in society is important, but in isolation, this is not enough in many cases to prevent people slipping back into criminal ways of thinking and acting.

A discrete category of positive diversion programs is those that attempt to redirect or transform criminal behaviour into noncriminal behaviour rather than suppressing it entirely. For example, a young person who engages in illegal graffiti may be diverted into a program that encourages legal 'urban art'. The key feature of this type of diversion is that it accepts and leverages the motivation for committing a criminal behaviour and provides a legitimate means to express it. This opens the door not only to a legitimate pastime, but also to the skills that can lead to gainful employment and exposure to noncriminal peers. Rather than simply using a diversion program activity as an angle or hook to attract and retain young people (as can be argued for sports and arts programs in general), here the diversion activity itself is directly relevant to the offending behaviour. Of course, this approach relies upon an understanding of a person's motivation and goals for engaging in the undesired behaviour and a feasible legal means to achieve those same goals—which may be more relevant to some types of offending than others.

This diversion approach has been widely used with graffiti offenders. Though we could not locate any robust evaluations for these sorts of programs, we will draw upon the limited literature in this area due to its potential applicability to cybercrime. Councils embracing this type of positive diversion have adopted strategies that allow artists to express their graffiti in a legal way (e.g. tolerance zones, commission of murals). In addition, some councils coordinate art workshops facilitated by senior street artists, providing positive role modelling, skills, and opportunities for young people to engage in art. Programs are usually run within community facilities where referral to other services is provided if necessary. Scholars, councils, and young people have indicated support for such programs, lending them some credibility (Halsey and Pederick 2005; Macdonnell 2015). Of course, pending robust evaluation, it is impossible to infer that urban art diversions actually reduce crime.

It should be noted that not all positive diversions using this logic have had success. The U-Turn program was developed in Australia to redirect young people from stealing cars by transforming the thrill-seeking that is associated with motor vehicle theft into legal, safe, and fun motorsport activities. The program, which targeted both low- and high-risk offenders, consisted of a course in car maintenance and bodywork, supplemented with case management, links to employment and further education, recreational activities (e.g. go-karting), and post-course support. An evaluation of one program site found that about two-thirds of participants self-reported antisocial behaviour while participating in the course, and at follow-up, 48% had recorded new offences (Kellow et al. 2005). Though there was no comparison group with which to compare this figure, the program did not strike policymakers as sufficiently effective, and they subsequently abandoned the scheme in favour of a psychotherapeutic intervention that addresses antisocial cognition and other criminogenic needs (Bolger 2015). Though the initial U-Turn program evaluation was far from robust, it does suggest that not all offences and motivations may be readily redirected into prosocial alternatives; in particular, higher-risk offenders may require careful and tailored targeting of criminogenic risk factors.

Moreover, the U-Turn program had *adverse* effects on some low-risk participants (Kellow et al. 2005), which may partially account for the evaluation findings. This raises the important issue of the need to keep low-risk and high-risk offenders separate in treatment programs (as per the RNR model). Placing groups of low-risk youths together with high-risk youths, even in a well-meaning spirit of diversion/prevention, can increase crime via peer contagion. When juvenile delinquents are placed together, they may reinforce antisocial behaviours and attitudes, which will be of particular detriment to those who are not highly deviant to begin with (Boxer et al. 2005). However, this is also a problem even when higher-risk youths are treated separately, as they can reinforce and amplify each other's antisocial attitudes (Cho et al. 2005; Dishion et al. 1999; Rhule 2005). Furthermore, by connecting with peers who have similar criminal histories and propensities, such interventions may simply offer an opportunity for young people to form deviant friendships or build cohesion among existing groups (see Braga 2016). In addition, Braga (2016) cautions that using ex-offenders in deviant peer programs is precarious, as by sharing their past experiences, former offenders may inadvertently glorify criminal lifestyles, reinforce group processes, and in some cases, they might turn back to crime themselves through the relationships they develop with group participants.

In summary, positive diversion programs vary substantially in their ability to reduce crime. Novel or exciting programs are more likely to be more appealing to young people, but it is imperative that these programs address criminogenic factors (e.g. antisocial personality and cognition) rather than relying on a 'feel good' approach—no matter how well intentioned these programs may be. In addition, group programming carries risks such as peer contagion. Cécile and Born (2009) recommend several possible strategies to reduce the negative influence of antisocial peers in crime prevention programs, including more structured activities (also see Rorie et al. 2011), familial involvement, and contact with prosocial peers. Other scholars warn that labelling young people as delinquents, even within well-intentioned prevention programs, may be another possible explanation for criminogenic effects (Gatti et al. 2009), which may be harder to overcome.

FUTURE APPLICATIONS AND ADAPTATIONS TO DIGITAL CONTEXTS

To date, there has been no empirical evaluation of positive diversion programming for preventing cybercrime. Nevertheless, it is plausible that one could redirect the skills used for cybercrime into prosocial avenues (e.g. cybersecurity). Some cyber-offenders have expressed interest in, or have transitioned to, legitimate cybersecurity jobs (Mitnick and Simon 2011; Opie 2019). Moreover, from anecdotal evidence it appears that (at least some) graffiti artists and cyber-offenders derive a sense of identity and pleasure from offending, while their crimes are characterised by a notable *status culture*—that is, they are rewarded by peers in their own communities based on the skills/talent they use to offend (for graffiti culture see Halsey and Young 2002). Thus, it is possible that cyber-offenders would benefit from diversion into cybersecurity programs or training, where their skills can be recognised and rewarded. There is, however, little empirical evidence that such diversion is common, or outlining what factors enable such a transition. Since there is no empirical evidence conclusively proving the effectiveness of such positive diversions, they may be worth trialling and evaluating. However, from a practical perspective, it might be difficult to obtain support from industry for such schemes, given the security risks presented (e.g. providing opportunities to offend, contagion of prosocial peers).

In addition, resistance training would be needed to encourage the ability to overtly reject peer pressure to engage in delinquency or crime as with traditional interventions. This could include messaging models for individuals to apply in their own lives or adapt to specific situations when appropriate. There are various ways this could be achieved offline. Linking security professionals and others who engage in hacking as a legitimate career could serve as a vital source of imitation and messaging to shape attitudes towards the negative outcomes associated with criminal applications of hacking and promote the benefits and importance of prosocial hacking. Such programs could be implemented via hacker/security conferences locally and nationally, as well as through 'maker-spaces' and 'hackerspaces' where individuals are encouraged to engage in experiential learning with others in socially inviting situations (e.g. Holt and Kilger 2012; Kinkade et al. 2013; Steinmetz 2015). Connecting individuals to prosocial peers through mentoring (see Chapter 5) could provide another source of messaging.

A programmatic threat lies in the fact that it is extremely difficult to identify all the various forums, websites, social networking sites, and communities where individuals may go for information related to malicious hacking. Additionally, it is difficult to ascertain the extent to which individuals espouse criminal values privately but display knowledgeable prosocial values in open spaces. Thus, interventions may benefit from partnering with prosocial cyber-offender (especially malicious hacker) websites and forums to encourage legitimate applications of hacking, downplay criminality, and promote prosocial values. Such partnerships, operating in conjunction with real-world programming, may be able to influence the formation of bonds with ethical hackers and minimise connections to antisocial or criminal communities.

The challenge of any such program lies in the fact that positive diversions provide ways to keep individuals engaged in prosocial activities and separate them from deviant peer networks. Research suggests cyber-offender online social networks are as influential as those in the real world, if not more so, due to the smaller proportion of the population who take an interest in computers and technology (e.g. Holt 2009; Leukfeldt et al. 2017; Marcum et al. 2014). In this sense, gains in programs will only be sustained if individuals continue to participate in the activity past a one-off program. Since the Internet is always 'open', it would prove difficult to keep offenders from connecting with delinquent peers online and diverted from offending behaviours at all times.

Similarly, addressing criminogenic needs is likely key to the success of positive diversions. For example, challenging the justifications espoused by cyber-offenders through moral reasoning and cognitive restructuring might be particularly useful for this population (Chua and Holt 2016; Morris 2011; Turgeman-Goldschmidt 2008). Yet there is little research as to the criminogenic family and personal circumstances that may affect an individual's engagement in cybercrime (but see Weulen Kranenbarg et al. 2018, 2019). More research on cyber-offenders' criminogenic needs is required if programs are to be appropriately targeted.

REFERENCES

Andrews, D. A., Bonta, J., & Hoge, R. D. (1990a). Classification for effective rehabilitation: Rediscovering psychology. *Criminal Justice and Behavior, 17,* 19–52. https://doi.org/10.1177/0093854890017001004.

Andrews, D. A., Zinger, I., Hoge, R. D., Bonta, J., Gendreau, P., & Cullen, F. T. (1990b). Does correctional treatment work? A clinically relevant and psychologically informed meta-analysis. *Criminology, 28,* 369–404. https://doi.org/10.1111/j.1745-9125.1990.tb01330.x.

Bandura, A. (1971). *Social learning theory.* New York, NY: General Learning.

Bernburg, J. G., Krohn, M. D., & Rivera, C. J. (2006). Official labeling, criminal embeddedness, and subsequent delinquency: A longitudinal test of labeling theory. *Journal of Research in Crime and Delinquency, 43,* 67–88. https://doi.org/10.1177/0022427805280068.

Bolger, R. (2015, October 5). Tasmanian youth rehabilitation program to target criminal thinking. *ABC News.* Retrieved from http://www.abc.net.au/news/2015-10-05/youth-rehabilitation-program-targets-criminal-thinking/6827754. Accessed 28 May 2019.

Boxer, P., Guerra, N. G., Huesmann, L. R., & Morales, J. (2005). Proximal peer-level effects of a small-group selected prevention on aggression in elementary school children: An investigation of the peer contagion hypothesis. *Journal of Abnormal Child Psychology*, *33*, 325–388. https://doi.org/10.1007/s10802-005-3568-2.

Braga, A. A. (2016). The continued importance of measuring potentially harmful impacts of crime prevention programs: The academy of experimental criminology 2014 Joan McCord lecture. *Journal of Experimental Criminology*, *12*, 1–20. https://doi.org/10.1007/s11292-016-9252-4.

Cécile, M., & Born, M. (2009). Intervention in juvenile delinquency: Danger of iatrogenic effects? *Children and Youth Services Review*, *31*, 1217–1221. https://doi.org/10.1016/j.childyouth.2009.05.015.

Chandler, M. J. (1973). Egocentrism and antisocial behavior: The assessment and training of social perspective-taking skills. *Developmental Psychology*, *9*, 326–332. https://doi.org/10.1037/h0034974.

Cho, H., Hallfors, D., & Sanchez, V. (2005). Evaluation of a high school peer group intervention for at risk youth. *Journal of Abnormal Child Psychology*, *33*, 363–374. https://doi.org/10.1007/s10802-005-3574-4.

Chua, Y. T., & Holt, T. J. (2016). A cross-national examination for the techniques of neutralization to account for hacking behaviors. *Victims and Offenders*, *11*, 534–555. https://doi.org/10.1080/15564886.2015.1121944.

Coalter, F. (2013). *Sport for development: What game are we playing?* London, UK: Routledge. https://doi.org/10.4324/9780203861257.

Dishion, T. J., McCord, J., & Poulin, F. (1999). When interventions harm: Peer groups and problem behavior. *American Psychologist*, *54*, 755–764. https://doi.org/10.1037//0003-066x.54.9.755.

Drake, E. K., Aos, S., & Miller, M. G. (2009). Evidence-based public policy options to reduce crime and criminal justice costs: Implications in Washington State. *Victims and Offenders*, *4*, 170–196. https://doi.org/10.1080/15564880802612615.

Felson, R. B., & Staff, J. (2006). Explaining the academic performance-delinquency relationship. *Criminology*, *44*, 299–320. https://doi.org/10.1111/j.1745-9125.2006.00050.x.

Gatti, U., Tremblay, R. E., & Vitaro, F. (2009). Iatrogenic effect of juvenile justice. *Journal of Child Psychology and Psychiatry*, *50*, 991–998. https://doi.org/10.1111/j.1469-7610.2008.02057.x.

Gavazzi, S. M., Yarcheck, C. M., Sullivan, J. M., Jones, S. C., & Khurana, A. (2008). Global risk factors and the prediction of recidivism rates in a sample of first-time misdemeanant offenders. *International Journal of Offender Therapy and Comparative Criminology*, *52*, 330–345. https://doi.org/10.1177/0306624x07305481.

Grieger, L., & Hosser, D. (2014). Which risk factors are really predictive? An analysis of Andrews and Bonta's "Central Eight" risk factors for recidivism in

German youth correctional facility inmates. *Criminal Justice and Behavior, 41,* 613–634. https://doi.org/10.1177/0093854813511432.

Haines, K., & Case, S. (2015). *Positive youth justice: Children first, offenders second.* Bristol, UK: Policy Press. https://doi.org/10.2307/j.ctt1t899qx.

Haines, A., Goldson, B., Haycox, A., Houten, R., Lane, S., McGuire, J., et al. (2012). *Evaluation of the Youth Justice Liaison and Diversion (YJLD) pilot scheme final report.* Liverpool, UK: University of Liverpool.

Halsey, M., & Pederick, B. (2005). *City of Melbourne draft graffiti management strategy, 2005: Graffiti writers' perspectives.*

Halsey, M., & Young, A. (2002). *Graffiti culture research report.*

Hirschi, T. (1969). *Causes of delinquency.* Berkeley: University of California Press.

Holt, T. J. (2009). Lone hacks or group cracks: Examining the social organization of computer hackers. In F. Schmalleger & M. Pittaro (Eds.), *Crimes of the Internet* (pp. 336–355). Upper Saddle River, NJ: Pearson Prentice Hall.

Holt, T. J., & Kilger, M. (2012). Know Your Enemy: The social dynamics of hacking. *The Honeypot Project.* Retrieved from https://www.honeynet.org/papers/socialdynamics. Accessed 28 May 2019.

Kellow, A., Julian, R., & Alessandrini, M. (2005). *Young recidivist car theft offender program (U-Turn). Local evaluation—Tasmania: Final report.* Hobart, Australia: Tasmanian Institute of Law Enforcement Studies.

Kinkade, P. T., Bachmann, M., & Bachmann, B. S. (2013). Hacker Woodstock: Observations on an off-line cyber culture at the chaos communication camp 2011. In T. J. Holt (Ed.), *Crime on-line: Correlates, causes, and context* (2nd ed., pp. 19–60). Raleigh, NC: Carolina Academic Press.

Koehler, J. A., Lösel, F., Akoensi, T. D., & Humphreys, D. K. (2013). A systematic review and meta-analysis on the effects of young offender treatment programs in Europe. *Journal of Experimental Criminology, 9,* 19–43. https://doi.org/10.1007/s11292-012-9159-7.

Leukfeldt, R., Kleemans, E. R., & Stol, W. (2017). Origin, growth, and criminal capabilities of cybercriminal networks: An international empirical analysis. *Crime, Law and Social Change, 67,* 39–53. https://doi.org/10.1007/s10611-016-9663-1.

Lipsey, M. W. (2009). The primary factors that characterize effective interventions with juvenile offenders: A meta-analytic overview. *Victims and Offenders, 4,* 124–147. https://doi.org/10.1080/15564880802612573.

Lipsey, M. W., & Derzon, J. H. (1998). Predictors of serious delinquency in adolescence and early adulthood: A synthesis of longitudinal research. In R. Loeber & D. P. Farrington (Eds.), *Serious and violent offenders: Risk factors and successful interventions* (pp. 86–105). Thousand Oaks, CA: Sage. https://doi.org/10.4135/9781452243740.n6.

Macdonnell, J. (2015). *An evaluation of its Street Art and associated graffiti prevention programs for Marrickville Council.* Sydney, Australia: Anzarts Institute.

Maguin, E., & Loeber, R. (1996). Academic performance and delinquency. *Crime and Justice, 20,* 145–264. https://doi.org/10.1086/449243.

Marcum, C. D., Higgins, G. E., Ricketts, M. L., & Wolfe, S. E. (2014). Hacking in high school: Cybercrime perpetration by juveniles. *Deviant Behavior*, *35*, 581–591. https://doi.org/10.1080/01639625.2013.867721.

McGrath, A., & Thompson, A. P. (2012). The relative predictive validity of the static and dynamic domain scores in risk-need assessment of juvenile offenders. *Criminal Justice and Behavior*, *39*, 250–263. https://doi.org/10.1177/0093854811431917.

Meade, B., & Steiner, B. (2010). The total effects of boot camps that house juveniles: A systematic review of the evidence. *Journal of Criminal Justice*, *38*, 841–853. https://doi.org/10.1016/j.jcrimjus.2010.06.007.

Mitnick, K. D., & Simon, W. L. (2011). *Ghost in the wires: My adventures as the world's most wanted hacker*. New York, NY: Little, Brown.

Morris, R. G. (2011). Computer hacking and the techniques of neutralization: An empirical assessment. In T. J. Holt & B. H. Schell (Eds.), *Corporate hacking and technology-driven crime: Social dynamics and implications* (pp. 1–17). Hershey, PA: IGI Global. https://doi.org/10.4018/9781616928056.ch001.

Morris, L., Sallybanks, J., & Willis, K. (2003). *Sport, physical activity and antisocial behaviour in youth* (Research and Public Policy Series No. 49). Canberra, Australia: Australian Institute of Criminology.

Opie, R. (2019, May 27). Adelaide teen hacked into Apple twice hoping the tech giant would offer him a job. *ABC News*. Retrieved from https://www.abc.net.au/news/2019-05-27/adelaide-teenager-hacked-into-apple-twice-in-two-years/11152492. Accessed 6 June 2019.

Petrosino, A., Turpin-Petrosino, C., & Guckenburg, S. (2010). Formal system processing of juveniles: Effects on delinquency. *Campbell Systematic Reviews*, *1*. https://doi.org/10.4073/csr.2010.1.

Rapp-Paglicci, L. A., Ersing, R., & Rowe, W. (2006). The effects of cultural arts programs on at-risk youth: Are there more than anecdotes and promises? *Journal of Social Service Research*, *33*, 51–56. https://doi.org/10.1300/J079v33n02_05.

Rhule, D. M. (2005). Take care to do no harm: Harmful interventions for youth problem behavior. *Professional Psychology: Research and Practice*, *36*, 618–625. https://doi.org/10.1037/0735-7028.36.6.618.

Rorie, M., Gottfredson, D. C., Cross, A., Wilson, D., & Connell, N. M. (2011). Structure and deviancy training in after-school programs. *Journal of Adolescence*, *34*, 105–117. https://doi.org/10.1016/j.adolescence.2010.01.007.

Schwalbe, C. S., Gearing, R. E., MacKenzie, M. J., Brewer, K. B., & Ibrahim, R. (2012). A meta-analysis of experimental studies of diversion programs for juvenile offenders. *Clinical Psychology Review*, *32*, 26–33. https://doi.org/10.1016/j.cpr.2011.10.002.

Seroczynski, A. D., Evans, W. N., Jobst, A. D., Horvath, L., & Carozza, G. (2016). Reading for Life and adolescent re-arrest: Evaluating a unique juvenile diversion program. *Journal of Policy Analysis and Management*, *35*, 662–682. https://doi.org/10.1002/pam.21916.

Simourd, L., & Andrews, D. A. (1994). Correlates of delinquency: A look at gender differences. *Forum on Corrections Research, 6*, 26–31.

Smith, P., Gendreau, P., & Goggin, C. (2002). *The effects of prison sentences and intermediate sanctions on recidivism: General effects and individual differences.* Ottawa, ON: Solicitor General Canada.

Smith, R. (2014). Re-inventing diversion. *Youth Justice, 14*, 109–121. https://doi.org/10.1177/1473225414537567.

Spruit, A., van Vugt, E., van der Put, C., van der Stouwe, T., & Stams, G.-J. (2016). Sports participation and juvenile delinquency: A meta-analytic review. *Journal of Youth and Adolescence, 45*, 655–671. https://doi.org/10.1007/s10964-015-0389-7.

Steinmetz, K. F. (2015). Craft(y)ness: An ethnographic study of hacking. *British Journal of Criminology, 55*, 125–145. https://doi.org/10.1093/bjc/azu061.

Turgeman-Goldschmidt, O. (2008). Meanings that hackers assign to their being a hacker. *International Journal of Cyber Criminology, 2*, 382.

Turner, J. C., & Oakes, P. J. (1986). The significance of the social identity concept for social psychology with reference to individualism, interactionism and social influence. *British Journal of Social Psychology, 25*, 237–252. https://doi.org/10.1111/j.2044-8309.1986.tb00732.x.

Uggen, C., & Wakefield, S. (2005). Young adults reentering the community from the criminal justice system: The challenge. In D. W. Osgood, E. M. Foster, C. Flanagan, & G. R. Ruth (Eds.), *On your own without a net: The transition to adulthood for vulnerable populations* (pp. 114–144). Chicago, IL: University of Chicago Press. https://doi.org/10.7208/chicago/9780226637853.001.0001.

Weulen Kranenbarg, M., Holt, T. J., & Van Gelder, J. L. (2019). Offending and victimization in the digital age: Comparing correlates of cybercrime and traditional offending-only, victimization-only and the victimization-offending overlap. *Deviant Behavior, 40*, 40–55. https://doi.org/10.1080/01639625.2017.1411030.

Weulen Kranenbarg, M., Ruiter, S., van Gelder, J.-L., & Bernasco, W. (2018). Cyber-offending and traditional offending over the life-course: An empirical comparison. *Journal of Developmental and Life-Course Criminology, 4*(3), 343–364. https://doi.org/10.1007/s40865-018-0087-8.

Wilson, H. A., & Hoge, R. D. (2013). The effect of youth diversion programs on recidivism: A meta-analytic review. *Criminal Justice and Behavior, 40*, 497–518. https://doi.org/10.1177/0093854812451089.

Wilson, S. J., & Lipsey, M. W. (2000). Wilderness challenge programs for delinquent youth: A meta-analysis of outcome evaluations. *Evaluation and Program Planning, 23*, 1–12. https://doi.org/10.1016/S0149-7189(99)00040-3.

Wilson, D. B., MacKenzie, D. L., & Mitchell, F. N. (2005). Effects of correctional boot camps on offending. *Campbell Systematic Reviews, 6*. https://doi.org/10.1177/000271620157800108.

CHAPTER 8

Restorative Justice

Abstract This chapter investigates a series of interventions that fall under the banner of restorative justice procedures. These procedures offer an informal alternative to formal court processes and typically involve bringing the offender and the victim together to discuss the harm caused, as well as measures to remediate the harm and assist the offender to avoid future offending. Restorative justice is influenced by re-integrative shaming theory, which argues that holding offenders accountable for their crimes in a socially re-integrative way can facilitate reconciliation and healing. We review the research literature, finding that the evidence for restorative justice interventions in reducing recidivism for traditional crimes is mixed and, overall, weak. To date, there are no studies that have empirically assessed the use of restorative justice practices in relation to cybercrimes of any kind, though some scholars have speculated as to their potential applicability. We outline the difficulties of applying restorative justice interventions to the online context and formulate a proposal for best-practice restorative justice procedures for cybercrime.

Keywords Family group conferencing · Procedural justice ·
Restorative justice · Reintegrative shaming theory · Sentencing circles ·
Victim-offender mediation

© The Author(s) 2019   109
R. Brewer et al., *Cybercrime Prevention*,
Crime Prevention and Security Management,
https://doi.org/10.1007/978-3-030-31069-1_8

INTRODUCTION

In this chapter, we consider the scope for the application of restorative justice practices to cases of cybercrime. Restorative justice has been defined as a 'voluntary, community-based response to criminal behaviour that attempts to bring together the victim, the offender, and the community, in an effort to address the harm caused by the criminal behaviour' (Latimer et al. 2005, p. 131). Its focus, simply put, is *restoration* rather than *punishment*. In most understandings of restorative justice, restoration refers to assisting offenders as well as victims. This is one reason why it has had extensive application to younger offenders and mainly in relation to less serious forms of crime (Sherman and Strang 2007): in contrast to formal criminal court processes, restorative justice generally has a stronger victim orientation.

We begin this chapter by exploring the theoretical background and rationale for restorative justice practices, before examining their effectiveness in preventing criminal activity. As we will demonstrate, there is very little empirical evidence to date of restorative justice for cybercrimes, although some anecdotal evidence of its trial use can be found. Thus, we shall examine the evidence of restorative justice's efficacy for offline crimes, focusing on differences between crime types as well as qualitative differences in the way restorative justice conferences are conducted. Given the key findings in the broader literature, we then discuss the applicability of restorative justice to the online context, accompanied by recommendations on best practice for the deployment of such interventions.

THEORETICAL UNDERPINNINGS OF THE INTERVENTION

Restorative justice is strongly linked to Braithwaite's theory of *re-integrative shaming* (Braithwaite 1989) and associated conferencing practices, appearing first in Australia. Re-integrative shaming posits the idea, based upon several other criminological theories, that justice procedures should aim to assist offenders to acknowledge the harm they have caused (shaming) but also treat them in ways that re-integrate them into the community. More recently, a connection to *procedural justice* and the work of Tyler (1990) has been acknowledged. This body of work considers restorative justice procedures to more likely be viewed as legitimate by offenders if they are treated with procedural fairness, where it is acknowledged that they have a right to participate in the process and to have their perspective considered. Legitimacy, in turn, is likely to be associated with a number of positive outcomes, including reduced recidivism.

Given the breadth and vagueness of its definition, it is not surprising that restorative justice has assumed various forms and thus been implemented in a variety of ways. Most typically, restorative justice is discussed in relation to (at least) one of three particular forms: *family group conferencing* (conferencing, hereafter); *victim-offender mediation* (VOM); and *sentencing circles* (Wong et al. 2016; Lauwaert and Aertsen 2015). These forms can exist either as alternatives (diversions from), or as supplements to, formal criminal justice processes. This means that restorative justice can occur prior to, instead of, during, or after the formal criminal process, including post-conviction with sentenced prisoners.

As noted, restorative justice events are intended to operate with less formality than court-based proceedings. Despite taking a variety of forms, there are some common features. Restorative justice events tend to be single meetings of varying duration: from less than one hour to several hours (see, e.g., McGarrell and Hipple 2007). In many cases, the parties will reach an agreement on remediation and other subsequent steps, usually relating to the offender agreeing to measures to reduce reoffending. Significantly, there will often be no monitoring or follow-up process after the event has ended. However, in rare instances, these tasks will be done by courts or some other agency acting under the court's direction.

Restorative justice events are chaired by a convener, a mediator, or a coordinator (hereafter, conveners). In some conferencing practices (e.g. the Canberra Re-Integrative Shaming Experiments [RISE]; Sherman et al. 2000), this person may be a police officer, though this is not a widespread practice. There is typically a period of pre-event planning in which the convenor contacts the parties to explain what is likely to happen and to secure their consent to participation, as well as arrange for supporters of both parties to attend (Strang et al. 2013, p. 47).

Participants usually include the convener, the victim, and the offender at a minimum. In some *mediations*, the victim and offender will not be present together (indirect mediation). However, co-presence is a feature and expectation of most restorative justice events. In *conferences* (as contrasted with mediations), parties beyond the victim and the offender are encouraged to participate, such as family members and supporters of the victim and the offender. In addition, one or more community representatives will be present. This may include a police officer or a representative from a non-government service provider. In *sentencing circles*, the event will normally be hosted by a senior community member. During the event itself, participation among those present will be facilitated by passing a 'talking piece' from one participant to another (Zehr 2002).

Offender acknowledgement of responsibility for the harm caused is a key component of restorative justice events. This sets the scene for the victim to speak to the impact of the crime and for the offender to respond to what the victim has to say. Expressions of remorse by the offender are highly prized. In restorative justice events involving young offenders, there will normally be a significant focus on the offender's response during the event and to their circumstances more generally. An apology or other expression of remorse will commonly set the scene for a pro-active attempt among those present to explore ways in which the offender can be assisted to improve his or her circumstances and to reduce the risk of further offending, as well as ways of remediating the harm to the victim.

As noted, the production of an agreement between the parties is a primary aim of these events (with the exception of VOM). These agreements, in addition to containing undertakings made by the offender to assist the victim or otherwise remediate the harm caused, may also record undertakings by others to assist the offender through referral to such things as treatment programs or educational or employment opportunities. This feature of restorative justice events points to the importance of restorative justice being nested within a broader supportive prosocial framework. Restorative justice, thus, can be viewed as one step along the pathway to desistance from crime (Claes and Shapland 2016).

CURRENT APPLICATIONS

Restorative justice interventions most frequently take the form of conferences and have been most commonly applied to young people, although they have also been deployed with adults. While mainly targeted at criminal offending, restorative justice has also been used to address student behaviour management issues in schools (Morrison 2007; Fronius et al. 2016) and workplace bullying (Braithwaite 2013). Much of the focus of restorative justice has been upon younger offenders as a diversion from formal processing, though it can also be used as a supplement to sentencing, or following conviction or a finding of guilt. In these cases, the court will monitor the outcomes of restorative justice events, and they can then influence the sentence imposed as well as the kinds of conditions specified as part of that sentence. Successful completion of a restorative justice agreement frequently leads to a reduced sentence.

While restorative justice is often targeted at first-time offenders, this is not always the case. One of the acknowledged challenges facing restorative justice is that it not be seen as an 'easy' or lax option by offenders or victims. In order to merit its use after subsequent incidents of offending by a particular individual, Braithwaite (2018) has argued there needs to be a level of escalating support in cases of reoffending, while making it clear to offenders that there will be a limit to how many times restorative justice will be used. In essence, he argues, there is the need to ensure that its extended application must come with the perception by the offender that the 'Sword of Damocles' (in the form of unavoidable punishment) will follow if restorative justice chances are not taken seriously (Braithwaite 2018).

As noted earlier, there have been no studies to date on restorative justice's application to cybercrime. In the offline context, however, it has been applied quite broadly to a range of crime types. As a general observation, restorative justice has tended to mainly be deployed in less serious forms of offending (Bergseth and Bouffard 2013, p. 1058), though it has also been applied to more serious crimes. Most frequently, restorative justice events have been applied to violent and property crimes (Sherman and Strang 2007), as well as being used to address sexual offences, public order offences, and alcohol and drug-related offences (Sherman et al. 2000). In post-sentencing situations, restorative justice has even been applied to homicides (Walters 2015). Nevertheless, there is some reticence about its application to more serious crimes because restorative justice can be viewed as delivering insufficient specific and general deterrence.

EVIDENCE BASE FOR INTERVENTION

Though we could not locate any empirical testing of restorative justice interventions for preventing cybercrime, there is a wealth of evidence in the offline context. In summary, the evidence for restorative justice's success in reducing reoffending across all types of crime is mixed. Results in terms of recidivism vary according to offence type, as will be discussed shortly. It is also easier to declare restorative justice successful on measures other than recidivism, such as victim satisfaction (Wilson et al. 2017). In their narrative review, Weatherburn and Macadam found 'little support for the hypothesis that RJ [restorative justice] is more effective than court in reducing re-offending' (Weatherburn and Macadam 2013, p. 14). One of the problems they observed in evaluating restorative justice effectiveness is a tendency for less serious, less persistent offenders to be directed to restorative justice, biasing findings of effectiveness in a positive direction (Weatherburn and Macadam 2013, p. 14). They also noted that more recent studies tend to be less favourable, as are those that adopt a more rigorous approach to evaluation.

Though several meta-analyses of restorative justice programs and practices have been conducted over the years, here we summarise only the most up-to-date and rigorous reviews pertaining to effects on recidivism. Strang et al. (2013) conducted a meta-analysis of ten randomised trials. They noted positively that nine of those studies showed less crime with restorative justice conferences than without them, though they also conceded that only one of the 10 indicated a statistically significant effect. The effect size found across the studies was, however, small.

Livingstone et al. (2013) undertook a meta-analysis review of restorative justice in reducing recidivism in young offenders 7–21 years of age. Based upon four randomised controlled trials only, they noted a high risk in most studies of a self-selection bias, as well as performance, detection, and attrition bias. They concluded that there was 'a lack of high quality evidence' regarding the effectiveness of restorative justice for young offenders and that there was no difference between those who were part of restorative justice conferences and those in normal court proceedings (Livingstone et al. 2013, p. 2). In relation to school-based offences, there is currently no strong evidence one way or the other in terms of restorative justice's efficacy (Fronius et al. 2016).

A more recent meta-analysis that took into account 60 randomised and quasi-experimental studies concluded that restorative justice programs and practices showed a modest reduction in future delinquent behaviour relative to more traditional juvenile court processing (Wilson et al. 2017). However, the authors noted substantial variability across the studies, as well as evidence of bias present in many of them. Across the 19 most robust studies (randomised designs), the overall mean effect size was reduced to a very small effect size that was not statistically significant.

Though restorative justice practices are often targeted at younger offenders, there are mixed findings in regard to whether the intervention is more effective when pitched at younger offenders. Hayes and Daly (2004) found that first-time offenders aged 10–12 years did better than older individuals (13–16 years) and that males were quicker to re-offend than females. However, in a comparison of youths and adults, Latimer et al. (2005) found no significant difference between the two groups in recidivism.

There is some evidence to suggest that restorative justice works more effectively with respect to some offence types than others. Some studies have suggested that it has greater impact on reoffending in cases of violent crime than property crime (see, e.g. Strang et al.'s 2013 systematic review). This systematic review examined studies of restorative justice dealing with both youths and adults. Unfortunately, this review expressly excluded from consideration two RISE experiments relating to crimes without personal victims—shoplifting and drink-driving (Sherman et al. 2015, p. 524). For non-victim crimes, the picture is less clear. For example, Shapland et al.'s (2008) UK study only considered offences with 'direct, individual victims' with the result that 'nothing can be said about offences with institutional or commercial victims' (Shapland et al. 2008, p. 36).

Given the remote nature of much cybercrime, the evidence with respect to non-victim crime (e.g. disorderly behaviour, nuisance offences, drink-driving) warrants close examination. There is relatively little evidence unfortunately to draw upon here. While one study claims a small effect size for offenders under the age of 14 years (McGarrell et al. 2000 discussed in Strang et al. 2013; Sherman and Strang 2007), there is some uncertainty given that some victim offences seem to have been included in the non-victim group. Further evidence against its efficacy in non-victim cases is provided by Sherman et al.'s (2000) finding that drink-driving offenders who were conferenced showed a small increase in offending compared to those who went to court, while in relation to juvenile shoplifters apprehended by store security officers, no difference was found in offending rates (Sherman et al. 2000). Further, Bergseth and Bouffard (2013) found that restorative justice was not effective for a category of miscellaneous crimes including curfew violations, alcohol and tobacco offences, drug possession, traffic offences, and disorderly conduct—which might be considered non-victim offences.

Their findings suggest support for a more selective and targeted application of restorative justice than is customary.

One of the possible impacts upon restorative justice's effectiveness, especially among young people, is its perceived lack of legitimacy (see Tyler et al. 2007). Sherman and Strang (2007) observed a strong negative reactivity towards restorative justice in their Australian study involving Indigenous youth shoplifters. They speculate that this reaction may only arise in relation to property offences because 'it is arguable … that a victim of property crime can be seen as part of an unfair system' (Sherman and Strang 2007, p. 75). It may be, as Sherman and Strang suggest, 'that some people who are told they have behaved immorally by other people they neither trust nor like will become more criminal in future, rather than less' (Sherman and Strang 2007, p. 75). As Braithwaite (2018, p. 85) recently put it, 'people who are well liked but not loved are not potent at inducing remorse. Nor are the police'. Perceptions of unfairness and injustice, it has been suggested, threaten to undermine the legitimacy of formal procedures in dealing with cybercrime, as well as other kinds of offending (Holt et al. 2018). We will return to this point further below.

Under these conditions, securing the participation of offenders in restorative justice can be challenging, especially with younger offenders. Their participation includes acknowledgement of the harm they have caused. Without this, there is little prospect of 'eliciting remorse for the offender and allowing the victim to articulate harm' (Rossner and Bruce 2016, p. 116). Some offenders might not see their activities as harmful, or if they do, they see their actions as justified. Others, often younger offenders, lack the linguistic competence needed to communicate an apology. Some young offenders also tend to view restorative justice in instrumental terms, seeing it as a 'softer option'. In this context, an effective apology or show of contrition will be unlikely (Sherman and Strang 2007; Hayes and Daly 2003). Remorse appears as an important component of desistance from crime (Hayes and Daly 2003; Piquero 2017; Tangney et al. 2011).

Addressing perceptions of fairness and justice is, therefore, important in improving the potential efficacy of restorative justice. Hayes and Daly (2004), in their study of 200 case histories of young offenders, examined the issue of variability within conferences. They concluded that reoffending is less likely among young offenders involved in restorative justice if they express remorse and where the agreements were the result of genuine consensus rather than being imposed upon the offender (see also McGarrell and Hipple 2007; Maxwell and Morris 2001). Shapland et al. (2008) found some significant relationships between adult offender assessments of restorative justice and a number of measures of reoffending. These included 'the extent to which the offenders felt the conference had made them realise the harm done' (Shapland et al. 2008, p. iv).

Increasingly, it is seen as unrealistic to evaluate restorative justice outcomes in the way other therapeutically intended interventions might be evaluated. One reason is the short duration of a typical restorative justice conference. Second, as Weatherburn and Macadam (2013, p. 14) have pointed out, restorative justice 'was never designed to reduce the risk factors known to be associated with involvement in crime'. Instead, restorative justice might be better viewed as a 'way of delivering multiple strategies' (Braithwaite 2018, p. 87) or, similarly put but in the language of desistance, an opportunity to 'facilitate a desire, or consolidate a decision [by an offender] to desist' (Robinson and Shapland 2008, p. 352). Hence, it has been suggested, restorative justice might be combined 'with correctional measures that have been shown to be effective in reducing re-offending' (Weatherburn and Macadam 2013, p. 14, emphasis in original), such as family therapy programs (Schwalbe et al. 2012, p. 30). Latimer et al. (2005) undertook a meta-analysis of 35 programs, 26 of which were youth focused. While restorative justice could be said to have delivered a statistically significant reduction in recidivism, it was clear that generally speaking, psychologically informed treatments yield much stronger impacts on reoffending (Latimer et al. 2005, p. 140). Linking restorative justice more effectively to programs of proven efficacy, therefore, makes a lot of sense.

FUTURE APPLICATIONS AND ADAPTATIONS TO DIGITAL CONTEXTS

The potential application of restorative justice to economic cyber-crimes, including online fraud, has been raised by a small group of scholars (Levi et al. 2015; Button et al. 2015). In a research report for the City of London Corporation, Levi et al. (2015, p. 70) state that while the small number of prosecutions of these crimes make the salience of restorative justice to this area questionable, it might have some value in responding to younger offenders or prospective offenders. They suggest that its value potentially is to be found in its ability to convey a message of the harmfulness arising from such crimes. Moreover, some victims of cybercrime have expressed interest in restorative justice responses. In an exploration of the views of online fraud victims, Button et al. (2015) encountered considerable interest among their victim group in the potential of restorative justice to offer two things. First, it would enable victims to learn about who had victimised them and how and why they had been selected. Second, it would enable victims to demonstrate to the offenders the harm they had caused the victims (Button et al. 2015, p. 208). Given the ready availability of rationalisations for malicious hacking behaviour among the cyber-offender communities (see Brewer et al. 2019), victim pressure for restorative justice may indeed lead to more opportunities in which harms can be explained to offenders and given a human face.

As already noted, however, there is no evidence to date of the application, or effectiveness, of restorative justice in the cybercrime realm. Given the pervasive interest in this domain by young people, and the widespread use of restorative justice particularly for cases of youth offending, this apparent gap is surprising. While the evidence for its efficacy in offline crimes is mixed at best, there remains a strong commitment to its improvement and its ongoing application particularly in the earlier stages of criminal trajectories. It seems unlikely, therefore, that this gap will remain for long as more cases of youth offending come to light.

We see several opportunities here. The prevalence of rationalisations among young cyber-offenders, especially those that downplay or deny harm from their actions, means that conferences need to provide credible counters to these views. Where offenders see their actions as warranted because the 'system' is unfair, their responses to official intervention (court or conference) may be ones of defiance or resistance. Overcoming this stance will probably require a sustained, concerted effort that cannot be delivered by restorative justice alone. Given the arm's-length—even anonymous—nature of much cybercrime, conferences will often provide the first opportunity to present an embodied victim to the offender. This will frequently challenge those facilitating and convening the conference because the victims will often be located in other jurisdictions. Videoconferencing will often be a practical solution for these situations.

Practitioners wishing to apply restorative justice to cybercrime will also face some key challenges. As with offline offending, the diversity of types of cybercrime makes generalisations of any kind about appropriate interventions difficult. As canvassed in Chapter 1, we still have limited understandings of cyber-offender characteristics. Furthermore, as flagged above, giving cybercrime a human face, especially by bringing offenders and victims together in the same physical space, will often prove difficult. Cybercrimes are typically committed remotely by offenders who never meet their victims. However, in some cases, there will be no 'victim' with a face. A malicious hack on infrastructure, for example, will undoubtedly inconvenience or harm many, but the harms are diffused, at least from the offender's point of view, across a largely unknown group of individual victims. How victims could be represented effectively in relation to such crimes is an important threshold question. Proxy or representative victims in other restorative justice settings have been seen as detrimental in terms of achieving the offender's buy-into the process, especially where the proxy is seen as dominating the discussion. Any persons who play this role would need to adopt a measured approach, one that shows some appreciation of the offender's circumstances.

As noted earlier, an important element of restorative justice is to have the supporters of the offender present as well as the victim. Harnessing the disapproval of those esteemed by the offender for his or her actions can assist in feelings, and subsequent expressions, of remorse. In terms of showing support for the offender, and providing assistance to him or her to adopt a more prosocial position in future, this is likely to prove challenging, again, given the isolated nature of some offending. Nevertheless, while more thought is required, there may indeed be ways of doing this virtually that overcome the physical separation yet remain effective (see Freitas and Palermo 2016). Moreover, the influence of peer groups is acknowledged in studies of how cyber-offenders are initiated and supported, yet researchers have thought little so far about the role of peers in assisting desistance and reduced reoffending in digital contexts. Where reinforcement for continued offending can be found online, as well as among one's offline peers, addressing peer influence (in terms of both recruiting prosocial peers to the restorative justice proceedings and considering external forces pulling on participants) is likely to be doubly difficult. Moderating features of the online environment, such as reducing perceived anonymity, as well as influencing their choice of offline peer associates, may be necessary. These measures of course are beyond the capability of restorative justice itself to implement or monitor.

The silver lining in terms of what restorative justice might positively contribute arises out of the fact that the skill set involved in many cybercrimes, especially of the more serious kind, has actual or potential application in legitimate fields of computer and software activity, as compared say to the skill set of a violent offender or thief. Therefore, there are potentially some proximal influencers and opportunities in these legitimate fields that could be incorporated into restorative justice procedures for cybercrimes (see Chapter 7). Obviously, there would be real value in tracking cases of this kind over time in order to gather evidence of efficacy.

REFERENCES

Bergseth, K., & Bouffard, J. (2013). Examining the effectiveness of a restorative justice program for various types of juvenile offenders. *International Journal of Offender Therapy and Comparative Criminology, 57,* 1054–1075. https://doi.org/10.1177/0306624X12453551.

Braithwaite, J. (1989). *Crime, shame and reintegration.* Cambridge, UK: Cambridge University Press. https://doi.org/10.1017/cbo9780511804618.

Braithwaite, V. (2013). *A multipronged approach to the regulation of workplace bullying* (Regulatory Institutions Network, RegNet Occasional Paper 20). Canberra, Australia: Australian National University.

Braithwaite, J. (2018). Minimally sufficient deterrence. In M. Tonry (Ed.), *Crime and justice: A review of research* (Vol. 47, pp. 69–118). Chicago, IL: The University of Chicago Press.

Brewer, R., Fox, S., & Miller, C. (2019). Applying the techniques of neutralization to the study of cybercrime. In T. Holt & A. Bossler (Eds.), *The Palgrave handbook of international cybercrime and cyberdeviance.* Palgrave. https://doi.org/10.1007/978-3-319-90307-1_22-1.

Button, M., McNaughton, N., Kerr, J., & Owen, R. (2015). Online fraud victims in England and Wales: Victims' views on sentencing and the opportunity for restorative justice? *The Howard Journal, 54,* 193–211. https://doi.org/10.1111/hojo.12123.

Claes, B., & Shapland, J. (2016). Desistance from crime and restorative justice. *Restorative Justice, 4,* 302–322. https://doi.org/10.1080/20504721.2016.1245912.

Freitas, P., & Palermo, P. (2016). Restorative justice and technology. In P. Novais (Ed.), *Interdisciplinary perspectives on contemporary conflict resolution* (pp. 80–94). Hershey, PA: Information Science Reference. https://doi.org/10.4018/978-1-5225-0245-6.

Fronius, T., Persson, H., Guckenberg, S., Hurley, N., & Petrosino, A. (2016). *Restorative justice in US schools: A research review.* San Francisco, CA: WestEd.

Hayes, H., & Daly, K. (2003). Youth justice conferencing and reoffending. *Justice Quarterly, 20,* 725–764. https://doi.org/10.1080/07418820300095681.

Hayes, H., & Daly, K. (2004). Conferencing and re-offending in Queensland. *ANZ Journal of Criminology, 37,* 167–191. https://doi.org/10.1375/acri.37.2.167.

Holt, T. J., Brewer, R., & Goldsmith, A. (2018). Digital drift and the "sense of injustice": Counter-productive policing of youth cybercrime. *Deviant Behaviour,* 1–13. https://doi.org/10.1080/01639625.2018.1472927.

Latimer, J., Dowden, C., & Muise, D. (2005). The effectiveness of restorative justice practices: A meta-analysis. *The Prison Journal, 85,* 127–144. https://doi.org/10.1177/0032885505276969.

Lauwaert, K., & Aertsen, I. (Eds.). (2015). *Desistance and restorative justice: Mechanisms for desisting from crime within restorative justice practices.* Leuven, Belgium: European Forum for Restorative Justice.

Levi, M., Doig, A., Gundur, R., Wall, D., & Williams, M. (2015). *The implications of economic cybercrime for policing.* London, UK: City of London Corporation.

Livingstone, N., Macdonald, G., & Carr, N. (2013). Restorative justice conferencing for reducing recidivism in young offenders (aged 7 to 21). *Cochrane Database of Systematic Reviews, 2.* https://doi.org/10.1002/14651858.CD008898.pub2.

Maxwell, G., & Morris, A. (2001). Family group conferences and reoffending. In A. Morris & G. Maxwell (Eds.), *Restorative justice for juveniles: Conferencing, mediation and circles* (pp. 243–263). Oxford, UK: Hart. https://doi.org/10.5040/9781472559111.ch-013.

McGarrell, E. F., & Hipple, N. (2007). Family group conferencing and re-offending among first time juvenile offenders: The Indianapolis experiment. *Justice Quarterly, 24,* 1–26. https://doi.org/10.1080/07418820701294789.

Morrison, B. (2007). *Restoring safe school communities: A whole school response to bullying, violence and alienation.* Sydney, Australia: The Federation Press.

Piquero, A. (2017). 'No remorse, no repent': Linking lack of remorse to criminal offending in a sample of serious adolescent offenders. *Justice Quarterly, 34,* 350–376. https://doi.org/10.1080/07418825.2016.1185530.

Robinson, G., & Shapland, J. (2008). Reducing recidivism: A task for restorative justice? *British Journal of Criminology, 48*(3), 337–358. https://doi.org/10.1093/bjc/azn002.

Rossner, M., & Bruce, J. (2016). Community participation in restorative justice: Rituals, reintegration, and quasi-professionalization. *Victims and Offenders, 11,* 107–125. https://doi.org/10.1080/15564886.2015.1125980.

Schwalbe, C. S., Gearing, R. E., MacKenzie, M. J., Brewer, K. B., & Ibrahim, R. (2012). A meta-analysis of experimental studies of diversion programs for juvenile offenders. *Clinical Psychology Review, 32,* 26–33. https://doi.org/10.1016/j.cpr.2011.10.002.

Shapland, J., Atkinson, A., Atkinson, H., Dignan, J., Edwards, L., Hibbert, J., et al. (2008). *Does restorative justice affect reconviction? The fourth report from the evaluation of three schemes.* London, UK: Ministry of Justice.

Sherman, L. W., & Strang, H. (2007). *Restorative justice: The evidence*. London, UK: The Smith Institute.

Sherman, L. W., Strang, H., Barnes, G., Woods, D. J., Bennett, S., Inkpen, N., et al. (2015). Twelve experiments in restorative justice: The Jerry Lee program of randomized trials of restorative justice conferences. *Journal of Experimental Criminology*, *11*, 501–540. https://doi.org/10.1007/s11292-015-9247-6.

Sherman, L. W., Strang, H., & Woods, D. J. (2000). *Recidivism patterns in the Canberra Reintegrative Shaming Experiments (RISE)*. Canberra, Australia: Australian National University.

Strang, H., Sherman, L. W., Mayo-Wilson, E., Woods, D., & Ariel, B. (2013). Restorative Justice Conferencing (RJC) using face-to-face meetings of offenders and victims: Effects on offender recidivism and victim satisfaction: A systematic review. *Campbell Systematic Reviews*, *12*. https://doi.org/10.4073/csr.2013.12.

Tangney, J. P., Stuewig, J., & Hafez, L. (2011). Shame, guilt, and remorse: Implications for offender populations. *Journal of Forensic Psychiatry and Psychology*, *22*(5), 706–723. https://doi.org/10.1080/14789949.2011.617541.

Tyler, T. R. (1990). *Why people obey the law*. New Haven, CT: Yale University Press.

Tyler, T. R., Sherman, L., Strang, H., Barnes, G. C., & Woods, D. (2007). Reintegrative shaming, procedural justice and recidivism: The engagement of offenders' psychological mechanisms in the Canberra RISE drinking-and-driving experiment. *Law and Society Review*, *41*, 553–586. https://doi.org/10.1111/j.1540-5893.2007.00314.x.

Walters, M. (2015). 'I thought "He's a monster"… [But] he was just… normal': Examining the therapeutic benefits of restorative justice for homicide. *British Journal of Criminology*, *55*, 1207–1225. https://doi.org/10.1093/bjc/azv026.

Weatherburn, D. & Macadam, J. (2013). A review of restorative justice responses to offending. *Evidence Base*, *1*. https://doi.org/10.4225/50/558114337730E.

Wilson, D. B., Olaghere, A., & Kimbrell, C. S. (2017). *Effectiveness of restorative justice principles in juvenile justice: A meta-analysis*. Fairfax, VA, USA: George Mason University.

Wong, J., Bouchard, J., Gravel, J., Bouchard, M., & Morselli, C. (2016). Can at-risk youth be diverted from crime? A meta-analysis of restorative diversion programs. *Criminal Justice and Behavior*, *43*, 1310–1329. https://doi.org/10.1177/0093854816640835.

Zehr, H. (2002). *The little book of restorative justice*. Intercourse, PA: Good Books.

PART IV

New Directions

CHAPTER 9

Designing and Evaluating Crime Prevention Solutions for the Digital Age

Abstract This chapter draws together the key empirical strands that have emerged throughout the preceding chapters and explicates the practical dimensions of this work. It acknowledges first that there has been very little research evaluating the effects of crime prevention initiatives on cybercrime. It then outlines ways in which this gap can be addressed in the future, and some of the issues that both researchers and practitioners will need to be aware of when it comes to implementing and evaluating cybercrime interventions. This chapter concludes by offering a number of recommendations for practitioners and researchers seeking to evaluate cybercrime interventions in the future.

Keywords Data collection · Evaluation design · Ethical issues · Generalisability concerns · Intervention evaluation · Maryland Scientific Methods Scale

As demonstrated across this book, to date there has been very little to no research evaluating the effects of crime prevention initiatives on cybercrime. Chapter 2 demonstrated that situational crime prevention (SCP) was by far the most commonly deployed cybercrime intervention, with some robust evidence (i.e. experimental and quasi-experimental studies) indicating that particular forms of SCP have showed some

© The Author(s) 2019
R. Brewer et al., *Cybercrime Prevention*,
Crime Prevention and Security Management,
https://doi.org/10.1007/978-3-030-31069-1_9

promise in effectively reducing cybercrime (albeit in limited contexts). These include the use of antivirus software, the use of warning banners, and the monitoring or surveillance of computer systems.[1] When it comes to other primary, secondary, and tertiary forms of cybercrime prevention, the other chapters in this book illustrate a far less developed evidence base. That is, there is only scant research available evaluating the effectiveness of such cybercrime interventions as universal communication strategies, educational workshops, mentoring, targeted warnings and police cautions, positive diversions, and restorative justice procedures. This lack of published research could be reflective of the relative novelty of cybercrime, a potential lack of interest by cybercrime researchers, or publication bias. In any case, despite there being a relatively robust evidence base for these interventions in offline contexts, the unique characteristics of the cyber environment, as well as cyber-offenders, necessitate that cyber-specific evaluations be designed and conducted.

Such research is pivotal to ensure that crime prevention strategies are achieving their crime reduction goals, delivering value for money, and that there are no unforeseen or undesirable consequences (Hutchings and Holt 2017). Just like clinical trials are necessary to ensure that medicines are effective at preventing and treating diseases, crime prevention initiatives should be rigorously evaluated to determine whether interventions are effective at preventing crime or reducing recidivism. Moreover, the existence of a rich evidence base can also make it possible to determine whether specific factors associated with an intervention have an impact on positive outcomes (e.g. who runs the intervention, who the targets are, the intervention's duration), as well as take stock of any other moderating effects.

Evaluations also provide other critical insights not immediately apparent. For example, as has been established in offline contexts, crime prevention initiatives can have unintended effects and may even cause an increase in offending (Grabosky 1996; McCord 2003; Sherman 1993; Welsh and Farrington 2001). We have discussed such potential unanticipated consequences across this book. For example, some of the

---

[1]We acknowledge that elsewhere, less methodologically robust studies have also examined the merits of other SCP approaches within cybercrime contexts, including the use of firewalls and passwords, vulnerability patching, police crackdowns, intrusion detection and prevention systems, honeypots, audit trails, website takedowns, fraud detection systems, and spam filtering (see further Chapter 2).

evaluations examining the effects of various interventions showed an association with increased criminal activity (see Chapters 4–7). As laid out in these chapters, the factors driving these trends are complex and multifaceted and may be a product of poor intervention planning or training, net-widening effects, peer contagion, or crime displacement among others. We are still learning about the potential unintended outcomes for interventions designed to disrupt cybercrime (see further Hutchings et al. 2016; Moore and Clayton 2011; Soska and Christin 2015), and additional rigorous study is warranted.

This chapter sets out to address this need for additional research into the effectiveness and impact of cybercrime interventions by charting a path forward for researchers and practitioners alike. It is not our intention to provide a detailed account of *how* to conduct evaluations. For this, readers should consult the wealth of available resources on this topic (see, e.g., Cook and Campbell 1979; Ekblom and Pease 1995; Shaw et al. 2006, among others). This chapter instead seeks to build on this work and flag some of the potential challenges likely to confront those setting out to evaluate both new and pre-existing cybercrime interventions. We argue that in order to successfully navigate these challenges, researchers and practitioners must specifically tailor their evaluations to suit digital environments, as well as acknowledge the distinctive characteristics of cyber-offending. This chapter concludes by drawing together key points emerging from the discussion and offers a number of recommendations for undertaking research in the field—a way forward—which we hope will promote both more widespread and consistent use of evaluations in future interventions.

Navigating the Cybercrime Intervention Minefield

We acknowledge that conducting robust evaluations is challenging, and that the digital realm presents many unknowns. Researchers and practitioners who seek to implement evaluations must be cognisant of the many pitfalls before them. In particular, they must be attentive to the study design selected, be mindful of data collection techniques and sources, as well as give due consideration to the limits inherent in such approaches. As noted across the chapters in this book, cybercrime interventions are not simply offline interventions in a digital context. As such, we argue that intervention research pertaining to cybercrime presents some methodological challenges that can be different to those previously encountered in offline contexts. These challenges, if not addressed at the outset, have the potential to compromise the integrity of an evaluation and also affect its feasibility. Such matters must, therefore, be considered when designing and implementing any evaluation of a cybercrime intervention—whether this be for new interventions that are yet to be deployed, or pre-existing interventions where an evaluative component is being added. These challenges are canvassed below.

Selecting the Appropriate Study Design

Given that there are so few available evaluations of cybercrime interventions to date, it is particularly important that future evaluations be rigorous. One of the underlying reasons behind the relative scarcity of empirical research in this area could be the absence of universally regarded methodologies and consistent measurement frameworks to provide organisations with practical tools for assessing the effectiveness of cybercrime interventions (Torres et al. 2006). As demonstrated throughout this book, such evaluations can potentially be designed and implemented at different points in the offending lifecycle and can assume various forms. This is not to say that all evaluations are created equal. Both practitioners and researchers must take care to select an appropriate study design that will best measure the effects of an intervention.

Evaluations differ substantially in terms of their quality and robustness. There are a number of ways that the effects of an intervention can be measured, and the quality and usefulness of these vary considerably. Those looking to implement any such evaluation—pertaining to cybercrime or otherwise—must acknowledge that the stronger the research design, the greater the confidence that can be placed in the findings. Through the development of the *Maryland Scientific Scale*, Sherman et al. (1998) set out to design a tool to guide practitioners and researchers along this path, and to demonstrate the breadth and relative strength of the different research designs available. The *Maryland Scientific Methods Scale* scores a number of evaluation methods from one to five, with five being the most rigorous (Sherman et al. 1998). Just as the concept of primary, secondary, and tertiary crime prevention originates from public health, this scale is similar to those used for clinical trials (Sherman et al. 1998). Details of the methods, along with example hypotheses, are presented in Table 9.1, adapted from Farrington et al. (2002). The ideal method is an experimental design (Method 5), with random allocation

Table 9.1 Potential hypotheses and research designs for evaluating interventions, using the *Maryland Scientific Methods Scale*

Method	Description	Example hypotheses
1.	Correlation between an intervention and a measure of crime at one point of time	Following the intervention, there will be fewer cybercrime incidents recorded
2.	Measures of crime before and after the intervention, with no comparable control condition	Those who receive the intervention will commit fewer cybercrimes than before
3.	Measures of crime before and after the intervention in experimental and comparable control conditions	Those who receive the intervention will commit fewer cybercrimes than before, but there will be no decrease for those in the control condition
4.	Measures of crime before and after the intervention in multiple experimental and control units, controlling for other variables that influence crime	Those who receive the intervention will commit fewer cybercrimes than before, but there will be no decrease for those in the control condition, after controlling for other factors that influence cybercrime offending
5.	Random assignment of program and control conditions to units	Those randomly assigned to the experimental condition will have reduced offending rates compared to those assigned to the control condition

to experimental and control groups, and pre- and post-intervention measurements. Ideally, experiments will have large sample sizes and long follow-up periods (Welsh and Farrington 2001). Methods 3 and 4 are quasi-experimental designs, which can be used when random allocation is not possible, but the experimental and control groups can be matched so that they are comparable. It should be noted, however, that the scale has some limitations. For instance, it is not well suited to scoring robust repeated-measures analyses (e.g. time series analyses). At the very least, the scale provides a simple measure of internal validity that illustrates the study designs best suited for making inferences about causal effects of interventions (Farrington 2003).

Evaluations can be introduced using post-intervention designs that take a retrospective approach to measure the effects of interventions that have already been delivered. Alternatively, evaluations can be designed to run as part of the intervention. A key benefit of a prospective design is that the evaluation can involve both pre- and post-intervention measurements. When it comes to the deployment of future cybercrime interventions, they should, where possible, be implemented with evaluation in mind. Previous interventions, such as the *LizardStresser* and *Blackshades* interventions described in Chapter 6, took place at scale when police had data that enabled them to identify those who could have offended, or might do so in the future. When further opportunities arise to deliver such an intervention, we recommend random allocation to control and experimental groups, so that the effectiveness of the intervention can be evaluated robustly.

Random allocation to experimental and control conditions is particularly useful when comparing different intervention types. The control condition could consist of 'doing nothing', proceeding to investigation and potentially prosecution; alternatively, a warning could be the control condition, and the experimental condition might be restorative justice, mentoring, or education. The use of a control group also enables the evaluation of the intervention, while controlling for other factors that could affect the outcome, such as an underlying reduction in the rate of crime. Furthermore, random allocation to control and intervention group controls for selection biases might have an effect on the outcome (Sherman et al. 1998). For example, police decisions to divert offenders from the criminal justice system are not random (Hancock 1978; Sherman 1984; Snowball 2008). Therefore, the outcome may have more to do with who they decide to divert, rather than the intervention itself.

Experimental and quasi-experimental designs can also be used to inform cost–benefit analysis to evaluate the effectiveness of the intervention (Welsh and Farrington 2001). Cost–benefit analysis expresses costs and benefits in monetary terms; its outcome being presented as a ratio of the cost of the intervention to the monetary value of the outcome (Dossetor 2011). Other approaches to evaluation include cost-effectiveness analysis, which expresses outcomes in non-monetary terms (such as the cost per crime avoided), and cost-saving analysis, which limits the evaluation to one stakeholder, without including wider social outcomes (Dossetor 2011).

Even the most robust experimental designs are subject to threats to validity. Particularly with cybercrimes, interventions are likely to be discussed online by recipients, which could result in a contamination effect. General deterrence principles mean that someone in a control group who becomes aware of the intervention delivered to the experimental group may also change their behaviour. Furthermore, cyber populations are frequently mischievous (Hutchings and Holt 2018). If they are aware that different interventions are being applied, along with requests to speak to a researcher, they could potentially conspire together when providing responses to influence the results of an experimental design.

Finally, to draw robust conclusions, any evaluation, be it experimental, quasi-experimental or otherwise, needs adequate statistical power. This is a large subject in and of itself, and while some researchers have sought to set guidelines on such (e.g. Welsh and Farrington [2001] propose that for experimental designs, there should be a minimum of 50 units in each category in order to balance the treatment and comparison groups on extraneous variables), the reality is far more complex than this. Statistical power is a function of several factors, including the effect size of the intervention—that is, how much the intervention reduces the outcome variable (crime). The smaller the expected effect size, the larger the sample must be to detect a statistically significant effect, holding everything else constant. Underpowered studies are also more likely to produce false positive results, that is, effects that are not real (Ioannidis 2005). Furthermore, if the experiment aims to identify if there are differential (interaction) effects, such as whether the intervention works differently for some populations than others, larger sample sizes are usually needed (Sherman 1984). Required sample size can thus be calculated by determining the anticipated size of the effect (Cohen 1992), or alternatively, the smallest effect size of interest—that is, the minimum reduction in crime as a result of the intervention that may be considered practically meaningful or important (see King 2001). For researchers and policymakers concerned with cost-effectiveness, for example, knowing the absolute number of cybercrimes averted by a particular intervention would be a key consideration to build into evaluation design. Yet, finding enough participants (that is, cyber-offenders) to conduct a high-powered evaluation that can answer such questions is likely to be challenging.

Sourcing the Best Possible Data

For evaluation studies, offending should ideally be measured both pre- and post-intervention. This is easier said than done. Criminologists have, for some time, acknowledged the considerable difficulties associated with measuring criminal behaviour, as compared to health outcomes, because the former is often covert and hidden (Green 1985). Researchers typically use one of several ways to measure crime committed by an individual. These include self-reported offending and official records or reports (Kleinman and Lukoff 1981), although victim reports are rarely used in evaluation studies. Alternatively, other data, including those collected through monitoring and observation, can prove fruitful (Mazerolle et al. 1998). Evaluation research can also draw upon multiple sources to achieve its aims. Depending on the intervention and its goals, an evaluation may appropriately leverage data on the behaviours of particular individuals, whereas others may instead measure incidences of crime and crime attempts before and after an intervention has been implemented. It is worth noting that regardless of the data type, intervention form, or measure used, there are data challenges and biases that a researcher must be aware of, and account for, at the outset. These potential hurdles, especially as they pertain to cybercrime, are elaborated upon below.

Evaluations can utilise *self-report data*, which can be collected through surveys, as well as interviews, and may cover a number of topics, ranging from the subjects' views of the intervention, and their pathways into and out of offending, through to other questions of interest to the researchers. Questions can be a combination of fixed option (closed) responses and open responses and can assess various measures relevant to evaluating an intervention (see Table 9.2). Self-report data can be particularly robust and offer unique quantitative and qualitative insights into an intervention that are not possible through other means. However, self-report data can be notoriously challenging to collect (particularly in cybercrime contexts) and can be prone to bias.

Self-report data are typically collected from offenders through the use of interviews with a researcher (face to face, telephone, or online), or via the administration of a survey. Interviews can take place at the time an individual is referred to or receives an intervention, as well as at intervals post-intervention. While interviews have the potential to produce highly detailed data, they can be incredibly time-consuming, inconvenient, and expensive to arrange and conduct. In online contexts, such problems may be exacerbated by the limited contact points available, as well as the inability for the researchers to build a personal rapport with participants to encourage follow-up. In addition, interviews, be that on- or offline, require that offenders provide informed consent, which means that the subjects must be able to opt-out without penalty. This can have negative repercussions for the evaluation's sample size (discussed further below). Given the desirable study design characteristics discussed above, the value-for-money proposition of interviews alone may be limited.

Table 9.2 Measures and data sources

Measures	Data sources		
	Self-report data	Official data	Observation data
Whether the offender received the intervention	X	X	X
The offender's perceptions of the intervention	X		X
Whether the offender had committed any offences before receiving the intervention	X	X	X
Whether the offender had committed any offences after receiving the intervention	X	X	X
If so, the frequency and nature of their offending, and how this has changed since receiving the intervention?	X	X	X
If so, the time between receiving the intervention and resuming offending	X	X	X
Why the offender became involved in offending?	X		
If the offender stopped offending, why?	X		
If the intervention changed the offender's perception of being caught	X		
Prior to receiving the intervention, did the offender realise the illegality of their activities?	X		
The offender's personal characteristics, such as age, gender, school level, employment status, and relationship status	X	X	

Surveys are also commonly used to collect self-report data. Surveys are generally simpler, quicker, and less expensive than interviews to conduct at scale. They can be conducted online via the provision of a web link, or by using a paper-based survey (complete with a reply-paid envelope). Paper-based surveys offer an additional benefit in terms of providing participants greater confidentiality, as there will be no possible leakage through their Internet history records or IP address logging. However, paper-based postage may result in increased inconvenience, as well as increased costs on account of postage and handling. Regardless of the deployment mechanism, surveys have notoriously poor response rates (particularly among offending populations, and especially for online cohorts), and require robust follow-up procedures on the part of the researcher to ameliorate this issue (see Bachman and Schutt 2016; Gideon 2012; Baruch and Holtom 2008). In addition, while survey instruments can be created to canvass a wide range of topics, the circumstances and complexity of cybercrime may also make survey instruments hard to design. For example, the diverse nature of online behaviour can make it hard to provide closed response options, or to compare severity or offence type across participants. Cybercrime surveys are also necessarily limited with respect to the kind of data they can collect (i.e. lacking the nuance surrounding a response that might be gleaned through alternate means). They are also vulnerable to other problems common across crime surveys. For example, offenders may exaggerate facts, report only selectively, or have difficulty providing accurate answers about what they did and when (particularly if spanning a significant period of time).

It is also important to note that self-report data, whether collected through interviews or surveys, can be biased. This can occur in numerous ways. The fact that the behaviour of interest is criminal may add problems of veracity, particularly if subjects are sceptical of the anonymity provided by the research design. For instance, prolific or serious offenders may be less likely to confess via self-report data, while those that do respond may misreport the frequency or severity of their activities (Florêncio and Herley 2013). Such bias can also be exacerbated by low response rates. Giving strong assurances of anonymity may be counterproductive if it simply makes the anonymity risk more salient. Finally, if interviewing participants in person, the researchers need to have some technical knowledge to have credibility with participants (Hutchings and Holt 2018). Few people combine such knowledge with the skills needed to interview offenders.

Those relying upon self-report data should be prepared for low response rates and potential participation bias (particularly for cyber-crime-related evaluations), and deploy active measures to combat this. Very little research on cybercrime offender populations has used a sampling frame (and hence been able to provide a response rate). Nevertheless, in one example, Hutchings and Clayton (2016) achieved a 25% response rate with their survey of booter service providers, but they sent up to four invitations to each subject. They also compared invitations to participate in an online survey versus an interactive online interview and found the former to elicit more responses (although those who took part in an interview answered more questions). In addition, the potential for attrition during follow-up periods should be considered (Farrington and Welsh 2005). For example, some individuals may not participate in self-report surveys during follow-up periods. Others may opt to have their data removed from the analysis, their whereabouts may not be ascertained, or they may have died.

Another important source of data is *official records/reports.* This involves examination of records held by government sources, such as through the criminal justice system, including police arrest records, offender databases, court, and other records (e.g. data collected from schools, corrections, social services, etc.). Such data have been used by criminologists for over a century for the analysis of crime and criminal justice trends. Criminal justice data can yield unique and potentially detailed insights into offending and offender characteristics that can be particularly useful in evaluating interventions. For example, such data can provide essential information about crime events, as well as offenders and their offending. It can contain information on all reported crimes, arrests, and convictions.

Many scholars have noted, however, that conducting research using criminal justice data presents numerous challenges. Gaining access to quality, usable data is arguably one of the greatest challenges facing researchers seeking to evaluate interventions. Such research requires the assistance of the relevant agency or body that maintains official records of contact (with the criminal justice system or otherwise). Data access would need to be negotiated and is by no means assured. Such access procedures may be labour-intensive, time-consuming and also potentially come at a financial cost. In addition, much official data have originally been collected for other purposes and must, therefore, be prepared for evaluation research. As such, any data extracted and used by the researcher would also first need to be searched, matched, and provided in a de-identified format suitable for analysis.

Researchers have also long understood that such data are both incomplete and limited (Becker 1963), which therefore frames the ways in which it should be understood, as well as limits analysis and interpretation. Notably, such data include only a sample of criminal events and offenders, including only those who have come to the attention of law enforcement. This makes the true extent of crime difficult to measure, particularly crimes that are less likely to be reported or are more covert in nature. Cybercrime is often a particularly hidden crime, and many offenders never come to the attention of law enforcement. Cyber-offenders may also be particularly likely to 'drift' into and out of offending (Goldsmith and Brewer 2015), and there may be significant gaps in time involved. Online offenders often believe that they will never be detected (Hutchings 2016), and in many cases, they will be right. This point is demonstrated using data collected by Hutchings (2019): those arrested, charged, and prosecuted for online offences were offending for an average of 1.7 years, and in some cases as many as 8 years, before being detected. This can be particularly problematic for research evaluating a cybercrime intervention, as failure to detect offending will have an adverse effect on the accuracy of the results of the evaluation.

Relatedly, when analysing official data, it is important to recognise that even if crime is reported, there can be many delays in the system that can impact the quality of the data. For example, Kleinman and Lukoff (1981) reviewed the criminal records of heroin addicts shortly after the end of their methadone treatment, and again two years later. They found that there could be a 'noticeable lag' in time between a crime and its entry into the official records. In a more recent example, Ringland (2013) compared estimates of reoffending obtained from police and court data. They found that the median time between reoffending and police commencing court proceedings was one day, while the time until finalisation in court was 86 days.

Measurements using official data do not suffer from the same participation biases as self-reported offending. However, researchers using official data must be aware of other biases. First, the data made available to researchers are unlikely to offer a complete picture of offending, but may instead be shaped by the assumptions, methods and priorities of the original custodians of the data (Faust and Tita 2019). Put another way, these custodians may have introduced their own biases into the data. For example, arrest data will be reflective of who is actually detected by law enforcement—which in turn may be influenced by choices made by police about which cybercrimes, individuals or online spaces (e.g. particular web forums or illicit markets) to target; what investigative techniques, capabilities, and resources are available; and staffing requirements. Cybercrime investigations and prosecutions can be long, costly, and incredibly resource-intensive. Therefore, choices are made about which cases are pursued and which are not (Smith et al. 2004). It is also possible that cyber-offenders who have been detected differ from those who have not. For example, they may be more prolific or more likely to attack high-value targets, or they may simply be less skilled.

In addition to self-report and official data, it is possible to *observe* 'ground truth' behaviours, through the monitoring of cyber-offender activities as they occur and analysing the data these behaviours generate. For example, law enforcement agencies around the world have experience in infiltrating and assuming control of forums and markets dedicated to a wide range of cybercrimes (e.g. Glenny 2011; Bleakley 2018). Elsewhere, cyber-offenders who buy or sell illicit goods or services using Bitcoin or other cryptocurrencies are particularly open to traffic analysis (Christin 2013). Such techniques could be used to evaluate interventions, including the random allocation of buyers and sellers to experimental and control conditions, and measure their subsequent activities. Some advance planning is likely to be useful here, as certain factors beyond the evaluator's control could potentially undermine results as will now be discussed.

It is possible, for example, that the users of a forum would discuss any intervention they received, potentially exposing the experimental design and compromising the evaluation. Indeed, discussions about interventions have already been observed on underground forums. Data collected for the CrimeBB dataset (Pastrana et al. 2018) from the popular online forum *Hackforums*, illustrated this following the *Blackshades* warning letter intervention (see further Chapter 6). Here, one user took to the forum and wrote:

What the actual f*ck! Got a letter from the NCA to my NEW address regarding the use of BlackShades... I never f*cking bought BlackShades nor did I ever use it due to hearing about it's ... backdoor. This is f*cking horse sh*t - luckily no arrest made but they've asked me to destroy it if I still have possession.. I never had f*cking possession.. I never touched that f*cking sh*t.. I'm not sure if others in the UK got this but this is bullsh*t. It's dated the 1st of July; it took 23 days to deliver this sh*t.. (Fun fact; I'm about 200 meters from a police station).. Yeah I blanked my first name; plenty of people know it; I know. I never touched BlackShades so I don't give a f*ck - I'm more bothered about how my name and stuff got in their database - they clearly got my new address due to me registering to vote ect. Plus I got nothing to hide so I didn't exactly hide it.

This post resulted in robust discussion and debate among forum users regarding both the merits of intervention, as well as speculation surrounding the processes by which the National Crime Authority (NCA) may have compiled its dataset. On this latter point, one commenter within the same thread suggested that someone else could have used the recipient's email address, which might explain why they had received the letter without having purchased *Blackshades*. Another provided an alternate explanation:

> Probably they busted the guy who made the blackshades and contacted paypal for the names of all the people who purchased it; then send the letter to all the names; hoping to scare them and make them delete it. Your name was going in the list probably because you purchased something rat-related (crypters).

As the result of such discussions, users who were not given the intervention might be deterred indirectly (no longer acting as an appropriate control condition), or users could displace to a different service that is not being monitored (e.g. another web forum or illicit market). In addition, it is entirely possible that police or investigative agencies endowed with this type of access may elect to use it for covert monitoring or high-profile arrests rather than for research purposes such as evaluating interventions.

It is also possible that the user above was in fact telling the truth. Sometimes those that are targeted for intervention may not necessarily be connected to any actual cybercrime activities. Evaluations relying upon observations or monitoring of cybercrime must, therefore, consider available data with caution, as the attribution of cybercrimes can be difficult to accurately discern. While there can be indicators as to who was involved in an incident, these can often be faked, particularly by more skilled offenders. For example, the mapping of IP addresses to subscriber information, which is often used for attribution, is not always perfect. Offenders can use VPNs, proxy servers, anonymity networks, or unsecured Wi-Fi connections. Attribution can also fail due to human error, such as incorrectly recording the IP address (Champion 2017). Most consumer IP addresses now change over time, so attribution depends on accurate reading and recording of time zones (Clayton 2005). Furthermore, account takeovers can be targeted in order to 'set up' a rival or take advantage of their status and reputation. There can be higher confidence when an incident is linked to a subscriber multiple times, or across multiple platforms. Where there is just one indicator, it is perhaps better treated as a clue than as definitive evidence.

Being Attentive to Ethical Issues

Researchers engaging offenders, victims, and criminal justice data must be attentive to a wide range of ethical concerns when designing, implementing, and analysing evaluations. There is an established literature exploring the ethical considerations in evaluation research (see Simons 2006), particularly across criminal justice contexts (see Weisburd 2003). As such, all of these will not be retrodden here. However, those evaluating cybercrime interventions should be attentive to certain ethical issues that may be exacerbated through digital environments, which could afflict such research. These include concerns regarding the potential for obfuscation of age (and other forms of disadvantage), as well as the chronic over-sampling of cyber-offenders by researchers.

The relative anonymity afforded by digital technologies and the Internet makes it difficult to draw firm conclusions about the composition of samples of cyber-offenders (Goldsmith and Brewer 2015), particularly in cases where observational or surveillance data sources are used. Unbeknownst to the researcher, targets of an intervention (and thus the evaluation) may be from vulnerable populations, such as children or adolescents (Holt et al. 2018), or suffering from a mental health condition (Schell and Melnychuk 2011). As such, it is possible that such individuals are recruited into a study without the necessary consent protocols being in place, or other risks and burdens being adequately addressed.

It is also important to note that as a whole, cyber-offenders are potentially subject to over-sampling by researchers other than those involved in a particular evaluation. Criminologists, for example, routinely collect and analyse content found online in their research (e.g. data scraped from illicit markets or web forums). These data are widely used because they can be rapidly collected at scale (i.e. through the use of a crawler), and is increasingly done without the consent or knowledge of site owners or content creators (Ball et al. 2019; Décary-Hétu and Aldridge 2015). As such, cyber-offenders may be the subject of a multiplicity of different research studies. Moreover, as cyber-offenders often have affiliations across multiple sites, their exposure may be increased further. Not only does this serve as a burden to participants, but there are also implications for data quality if it results in a higher refusal rate (i.e. a less representative sample) (see further Clark 2008).

Acknowledging Generalisability Concerns

As with most forms of empirical social research, evaluating interventions presents unique challenges to generalisability beyond the population being studied (Sherman et al. 1998). In addition to the routine generalisability limitations regarding the applicability of specific case studies to other jurisdictions or group contexts, and the implications from incomplete or missing data, there are other generalisability concerns that need to be acknowledged when undertaking criminal justice-related interventions. Such concerns can stem from the type of intervention and crime type, as well as offender characteristics.

Given the time and costs associated with developing and deploying robust evaluations, it is likely that the research design must necessarily be constrained. As was demonstrated throughout this book, evaluations are typically highly focused on a single intervention taking place in a particular context, and in relation to a single form of criminal activity (e.g. possessing a specific type of malware, as was the case in the *Blackshades* intervention). Given the diversity of cyber-offenders and cybercrimes discussed in Chapter 1, findings for one type of activity (e.g. DDoS attacks) may not hold true from other types of criminal activity (e.g. writing viruses or malware)—particularly given their different motivations, methods, and required skill sets.

Even within a sample of offenders, the effectiveness of an intervention may also vary by certain offender characteristics such as relationship status, employment status, education level, and race (Sherman et al. 1992). As such, particular characteristics of cyber-offenders may mean that interventions designed for other populations (offline offenders, or even other types of cyber-offenders) have different outcomes.

CHARTING A PATH FORWARD FOR RESEARCHERS AND PRACTITIONERS

In this final section, we draw together the key challenges identified in the above discussion and offer a number of recommendations for researchers and practitioners seeking to undertake evaluations of cybercrime interventions. Researchers conducting evaluations in digital environments must carefully consider the study design, preferably selecting one that is both robust, yet feasible to design alongside the intervention (in lieu of tacking an evaluation on after the fact). The randomised controlled trials described above are the most valuable of the studies that evaluate the effects of crime prevention in terms of the insights they can provide. However, they are also the most resource-intensive. Furthermore, when planning such an evaluation, researchers should particularly consider the length of any follow-up period. Welsh and Farrington (2001) suggest that a lengthy follow-up period is required to assess how long the effects of an intervention persist after it has ended. Grabosky (1996) also notes that there may be a 'reversal of effects'; even if an intervention leads to an initial reduction in crime, it may actually increase in the longer term. An evaluation could incorporate multiple follow-up periods to measure short- and long-term effects. Self-report measurements of offending behaviour could be taken at each follow-up and matched with official data on contacts with the criminal justice system.

Given the challenges, and potential pitfalls of obtaining quality cyber-crime data—be it through self-report or official data, or observation—researchers must consider innovative ways to collect data. One path forward would be to consider using triangulated data where possible. This could help to counter the potential biases cybercrime evaluation researchers are likely to encounter with each data type. In the process of data collection, researchers must be alert to ethical issues. For example, they must carefully build in safeguards, so as to ensure that the risks to vulnerable people or groups are minimised (e.g. have processes in place to appropriately work with children), and to mitigate the burdens of over-sampling cyber-offenders insofar as is possible. For research that requires access to official criminal history data, other processes are appropriate, such as having data-sharing agreements in place.

Regarding generalisability, research needs to provide clear and detailed statements about the intervention and its aims, the types of cybercrimes targeted, the limitations of the data, as well as pertinent offender characteristics that may have bearing upon results. Providing clarity on these aspects can facilitate clear statements on the generalisability of results for each discrete study and allow such results to be meaningfully compared against the results from other evaluations.

We conclude by emphasising that it is not our intention to dissuade researchers from developing evaluations of cybercrime interventions. Rather, we echo the call made at the very outset of this book: that rigorous evaluations will be critical to understanding the impact and effectiveness of new cybercrime interventions as they are deployed. While to date the available evidence base is scant, a tremendous opportunity awaits. It is our hope that the discussion and recommendations presented offer a useful path forward and a means by which to navigate this challenging undertaking.

References

Bachman, R. D., & Schutt, R. K. (2016). *The practice of research in criminology and criminal justice* (6th ed.). Los Angeles, CA: Sage.

Ball, M., Broadhurst, R., Niven, A., & Trivedi, H. (2019). *Data capture and analysis of darknet markets*. Retrieved from https://ssrn.com/abstract=3344936; http://dx.doi.org/10.2139/ssrn.3344936.

Baruch, Y., & Holtom, B. C. (2008). Survey response rate levels and trends in organizational research. *Human Relations, 61*(8), 1139–1160. https://doi.org/10.1177/0018726708094863.

Becker, H. (1963). *Outsiders*. New York, NY: Free Press.

Bleakley, P. (2018). Watching the watchers: Taskforce Argos and the evidentiary issues involved with infiltrating Dark Web child exploitation networks. *The Police Journal: Theory, Practice and Principles*, 1–16. https://doi.org/10.1177/0032258X18801409.

Champion, M. (2017, May 13). *This is what it's like to be wrongly accused of being a paedophile because of a typo by police*. BuzzFeed News. Retrieved from https://www.buzzfeed.com/matthewchampion/this-mans-life-was-destroyed-by-a-police-typo. Accessed 20 July 2019.

Christin, N. (2013, May 13–17). Traveling the Silk Road: A measurement analysis of a large anonymous online marketplace. In *WWW '13 Proceedings of the 22nd International Conference on World Wide Web*. New York, NY: ACM. https://doi.org/10.1145/2488388.2488408.

Clark, T. (2008). 'We're over-researched here!': Exploring accounts of research fatigue within qualitative research engagements. *Sociology, 42*(5), 953–970. https://doi.org/10.1177/0038038508094573.

Clayton, R. (2005). *Anonymity and traceability in cyberspace* (Technical Report No. 653). Cambridge, UK: University of Cambridge, Computer Laboratory.

Cohen, J. (1992). A power primer. *Quantitative Methods in Psychology, 112*(1), 155–159. https://doi.org/10.1037/0033-2909.112.1.155.

Cook, T. D., & Campbell, D. T. (1979). *Quasi-experimentation: Design and analysis issues for field settings*. Boston, MA: Houghton Mifflin.

Décary-Hétu, D., & Aldridge, J. (2015). Sifting through the net: Monitoring of online offenders by researchers. *European Review of Organised Crime, 2*, 122–141.

Dossetor, K. (2011). *Cost-benefit analysis and its application to crime prevention and criminal justice research* (Technical and Background Paper Series No. 42). Canberra, Australia: Australian Institute of Criminology.

Ekblom, P., & Pease, K. (1995). Evaluating crime prevention. *Crime and Justice, 19*, 585–662. https://doi.org/10.1086/449238.

Farrington, D. P. (2003). Methodological quality standards for evaluation research. *The ANNALS of the American Academy of Political and Social Science, 587*(1), 49–68. https://doi.org/10.1177/0002716202250789.

Farrington, D. P., Gottfredson, D. C., Sherman, L. W., & Welsh, B. C. (2002). The Maryland Scientific Methods Scale. In L. W. Sherman, D. P. Farrington, B. C. Welsh, & D. L. MacKenzie (Eds.), *Evidence-based crime prevention* (pp. 13–21). London, UK: Routledge. https://doi.org/10.4324/9780203166697_chapter_2.

Farrington, D. P., & Welsh, B. C. (2005). Randomized experiments in criminology: What have we learned in the last two decades? *Journal of Experimental Criminology, 1*(1), 9–38. https://doi.org/10.1007/s11292-004-6460-0.

Faust, K., & Tita, G. (2019). Social networks and crime: Pitfalls and promises for advancing the field. *Annual Review of Criminology, 2*(1), 99–122. https://doi.org/10.1146/annurev-criminol-011518-024701.

Florêncio, D., & Herley, C. (2013). Sex, lies and cyber-crime surveys. In B. Schneier (Ed.), *Economics of information security and privacy III* (pp. 35–53). New York, NY: Springer. https://doi.org/10.1007/978-1-4614-1981-5_3.

Gideon, L. (Ed.). (2012). *Handbook of survey methodology for the social sciences*. New York, NY: Springer-Verlag. https://doi.org/10.1007/978-1-4614-3876-2.

Glenny, M. (2011). *DarkMarket: Cyberthieves, cybercops and you*. London, UK: The Brodley Head.

Goldsmith, A., & Brewer, R. (2015). Digital drift and the criminal interaction order. *Theoretical Criminology, 19*(1), 112–130. https://doi.org/10.1177/1362480614538645.

Grabosky, P. N. (1996). Unintended consequences of crime prevention. *Crime Prevention Studies, 5*, 25–56.

Green, G. S. (1985). General deterrence and television cable crime: A field experiment in social control. *Criminology, 23*(4), 629–645. https://doi.org/10.1111/j.1745-9125.1985.tb00367.x.

Hancock, L. (1978). Police discretion in Victoria. *The Australian and New Zealand Journal of Sociology, 14*(1), 33–40. https://doi.org/10.1177/144078337801400113.

Holt, T. J., Brewer, R., & Goldsmith, A. (2018). Digital drift and the "sense of injustice": Counter-productive policing of youth cybercrime. *Deviant Behavior*, 1–13. https://doi.org/10.1080/01639625.2018.1472927.

Hutchings, A. (2016). Cybercrime trajectories: An integrated theory of initiation, maintenance, and desistance. In T. J. Holt (Ed.), *Crime online: Correlates, causes, and context* (pp. 117–140). Durham, UK: Caroline Academic Press.

Hutchings, A. (2019). *Cambridge Computer Crime Database*. Retrieved from http://www.cl.cam.ac.uk/~ah793/cccd.html. Accessed 2 January 2018.

Hutchings, A., & Clayton, R. (2016). Exploring the provision of online booter services. *Deviant Behavior, 37*(10), 1163–1178. https://doi.org/10.1080/0 1639625.2016.1169829.

Hutchings, A., Clayton, R., & Anderson, R. (2016, June 1–3). Taking down websites to prevent crime. In *2016 APWG Symposium on Electronic Crime Research (eCrime)*. IEE. https://doi.org/10.1109/eCRIME.2016.7487947.

Hutchings, A., & Holt, T. J. (2017). The online stolen data market: Disruption and intervention approaches. *Global Crime, 18*(1), 11–30. https://doi.org/1 0.1080/17440572.2016.1197123.

Hutchings, A., & Holt, T. J. (2018). Interviewing cybercrime offenders. *Journal of Qualitative Criminal Justice & Criminology, 7*(1), 75–94.

Ioannidis, J. P. (2005). Why most published research findings are false. *PLoS Med. 2*, e124. https://doi.org/10.1371/journal.pmed.0020124.

King, M. (2001). A point of minimal important difference (MID): A critique of terminology and methods. *Expert Review of Pharmacoeconomics and Outcomes Research, 11*(2), 171–184. https://doi.org/10.1586/erp.11.9.

Kleinman, P. H., & Lukoff, I. F. (1981). Official crime data. *Criminology, 19*(3), 449–454. https://doi.org/10.1111/j.1745-9125.1981.tb00429.x.

Mazerolle, L. G., Roehl, J., & Kadleck, C. (1998). Controlling social disorder using civil remedies: Results from a randomized field experiment in Oakland, California. *Crime Prevention Studies, 9*, 141–159.

McCord, J. (2003). Cures that harm: Unanticipated outcomes of crime prevention programs. *The ANNALS of the American Academy of Political and Social Science, 587*(1), 16–30. https://doi.org/10.1177/0002716202250781.

Moore, T., & Clayton, R. (2011). *Ethical dilemmas in take-down research*. In G. Danezis, S. Dietrich, & K. Sako (Eds.), *Financial cryptography and data security workshop. FC 2011* (Lecture Notes in Computer Science, Vol. 7126, pp. 154–168). Berlin, Germany: Springer. https://doi.org/10.1007/978-3-642-29889-9_14.

Pastrana, S., Thomas, D. R., Hutchings, A., & Clayton, R. (2018, April 23–27). CrimeBB: Enabling cybercrime research on underground forums at scale. In *WWW '13 Proceedings of the 2018 World Wide Web Conference* (pp. 1845–1854). ACM. https://doi.org/10.1145/3178876.3186178.

Ringland, C. (2013). Measuring recidivism: Police versus court data. *Crime and Justice Bulletin, 175*, 1–12.

Schell, B. H., & Melnychuk, J. (2011). Female and male hacker conferences attendees: Their autism-spectrum quotient (AQ) scores and self-reported adulthood experiences. In T. J. Holt & B. H. Schell (Eds.), *Corporate hacking and technology-driven crime: Social dynamics and implications* (pp. 144–169). Hershey, PA: IGI Global. https://doi.org/10.4018/978-1-61692-805-6.ch008.

Shaw, I., Greene, J., & Mark, M. (Eds.). (2006). *The Sage handbook of evaluation*. London, UK: Sage. https://doi.org/10.4135/9781848608078.n11.

Sherman, L. W. (1984). Experiments in police discretion: Scientific boon or dangerous knowledge? *Law and Contemporary Problems, 47*(4), 61–81.

Sherman, L. W. (1993). Defiance, deterrence, and irrelevance: A theory of the criminal sanction. *Journal of Research in Crime and Delinquency, 30*(4), 445–473. https://doi.org/10.1177/0022427893030004006.

Sherman, L. W., Gottfredson, D. C., MacKenzie, D. L., Eck, J., Reuter, P., & Bushway, S. D. (1998). Preventing crime: What works, what doesn't, what's promising. In *National Institute of Justice: Research in brief*. Washington, DC: U.S. Department of Justice.

Sherman, L. W., Schmidt, J. D., Rogan, D. P., Smith, D. A., Gartin, P. R., Cohn, E. G., et al. (1992). The variable effects of arrest on criminal careers: The Milwaukee domestic violence experiment. *The Journal of Criminal Law and Criminology, 83*, 137–169. https://doi.org/10.2307/1143827.

Simons, H. (2006). Ethics in evaluation. In I. Shaw, J. Greene, & M. Mark (Eds.), *The Sage handbook of evaluation* (pp. 243–265). London, UK: Sage. https://doi.org/10.4135/9781848608078.n11.

Smith, R. G., Grabosky, P., & Urbas, G. (2004). *Cyber criminals on trial*. Cambridge, UK: Cambridge University Press. https://doi.org/10.1017/cbo9780511481604.

Snowball, L. (2008). Diversion of Indigenous juvenile offenders. *Trends and Issues in Crime and Criminal Justice* (No. 355). Canberra, Australia: Australian Institute of Criminology.

Soska, K., & Christin, N. (2015, August 12–14). Measuring the longitudinal evolution of the online anonymous marketplace ecosystem. In *Proceedings of the 24th USENIX Security Symposium, Washington, D.C.* (pp. 33–48). USENIX.

Torres, J. M., Sarriegi, J. M., Santos, J., & Serrano, N. (2006). Managing information systems security: Critical success factors and indicators to measure effectiveness. In S. K. Katsikas, J. López, M. Backes, & S. Gritzalis (Eds.), *Information security. ISC 2006* (Lecture Notes in Computer Science, Vol. 4176, pp. 530–545). Berlin, Germany: Springer. https://doi.org/10.1007/11836810_38.

6 R. BREWER ET AL.

146   R. BREWER ET AL.

Weisburd, D. (2003). Ethical practice and evaluation of interventions in crime and justice: The moral imperative for randomized trials. *Evaluation Review, 27*(3), 336–354. https://doi.org/10.1177/0193841X03027003007.

Welsh, B. C., & Farrington, D. P. (2001). Toward an evidence-based approach to preventing crime. *The ANNALS of the American Academy of Political and Social Science, 578*(1), 158–173. https://doi.org/10.1177/000271620157800110.

Index

© The Editor(s) (if applicable) and The Author(s) 2019
R. Brewer et al., *Cybercrime Prevention*,
Crime Prevention and Security Management,
https://doi.org/10.1007/978-3-030-31069-1

147

sentencing circles, 111, 112
situational crime prevention (SCP), 8,
    18–21, 23, 26, 125, 126
  definition, 6
  techniques, 8, 20, 27
social bond theory, 95
Social Networking Safety Promotion
    and Cyberbullying Prevention
    (SNSPCP), Arizona Attorney
    General's, 54, 55
spam filtering, 20, 126
sports programs, 98
spyware, 2. *See also* cyber-dependent
    crime, definition
Strengthening Families Program, 56
surveys, 21, 38, 40, 132–135

T
tertiary prevention, 4, 10, 38
  definition, 4

U
universal communications, 6, 8,
    35–39, 42, 43, 126

definition, 6, 35
U-Turn Program, 101

V
victim-offender mediation (VOM),
    111, 112
virus, computer, 2, 21. *See also*
    cyber-dependent crime, definition
vocational programs, 99, 100
vulnerability patching, 20, 126

W
warning banners. *See* warning messages
warning messages, 20, 21, 23–25
warnings, stand-alone, 78
website takedowns, 20, 126
wilderness camps, 97, 98

Z
Zatko, Peiter 'Mudge', 96

Printed in the United States
By Bookmasters